Front and back cover :
Feluccas at dusk on the Nile
Slide/Binder.

Flyleaf:
The Nile and the Pyramids
Hervé Champollion.

Page 6:
Personification of the Nile god Hapy
Temple of Ramesses II, Abydos.
Aude Gros de Beler.

Page 11:
Aswan: the Botanical Garden
Slide/Armor.

Pages 112 & 129:
Aswan: Elephantine Island
Hervé Champollion.

Photographic Credits:

Slide/Armor: 11, 38/39, 60/61.
Slide/Binder: 1, 71, 82/83, 85, 136.
Slide/Cash: 14/15, 20/21.
Slide/Hahn: 74/75, 76/77, 85.
Slide/Steffens: 16/17, 49, 79, 100/101.

Pix/Guiziou: 63.

Visa/Venturi: 65, 89.

Jean de Beler: 50/51, 92b,c, 93b, 95, 97.

Hervé Champollion: 2/3, 32/33, 34/35, 36/37, 41, 43, 44/45, 46/47, 54/55, 56/57, 69, 98/99, 103, 111, 112/129, 132/133.

Aude Gros de Beler: 6, 59, 66, 67, 73, 87, 91, 92a, 93a,c, 105, 107, 108/109.

Alain Mahuzier: 23, 25, 26/27, 29.

Nguyen Thuc Diem: 30.

Text: Aude Gros de Beler.
Collaboration: F. B.
Translation and Layout: DemiPage Services S.L.

THE NILE

Aude Gros de Beler

Foreword
Aly Maher el Sayed

THE NILE

Aude Gros de Beler

Foreword
Aly Maher el Sayed

FOREWORD

To follow the course of the Nile through geography and history is an incredible adventure. That is what this superb piece of work achieves: it constitutes a true voyage through Africa and through time; it takes the reader from the Ethiopian high plateau to the Delta of the Nile, from the Great Lakes region to the Mediterranean Sea... But it also invites us to travel down through the centuries of history of the civilizations who were born on the banks of the great river. For the Nile has been and remains a source of life, of prosperity and of civilization and it was along this river that the first State in the history of man was born, Egypt...

For the Ancients, it was more than a course of water; it was a god, a river-god, a divinity which they adored and respected, a continuous miracle... Since the beginning of time, this river, one of the largest in the world, has indeed intrigued men... What was the mystery of this river whose waters never dried up? Of this benevolent flood that renewed itself every year with an astonishing regularity? What divine source fed these waters? What was the secret of its fertile silt? For ages, men believed that the river descended from Heaven and the God Hapy, who personified it, and was among the most venerated gods in Egyptian mythology. Over the centuries, the greatest explorers dreamed of discovering its sources and set off in search of them... The Nile has been witness to history; it has seen empires, conquerors and warriors pass, but also men and women who, thanks to its waters, cultivated the earth and created life.

All along its 4,187 miles, the Nile changes its allure and character; it becomes with every turn, more powerful, impetuous and bold, before attaining peace and serenity, before pouring into the blue waters of the Mediterranean Sea... But it will always remain resolute and majestic, as it passes through tropical forests, harsh steppes or arid deserts... Throughout its course, the Nile displays a great beauty and a captivating charm... and nothing equals a promenade by a full moon, in a Felucca, or a dream-like cruise on its silvery waters, thus being touched by the magic of a river which has been sung by the greatest poets.

Egypt is indeed "a gift of the Nile" and all Egyptians are proud to be part of this river valley, unique in the world... and even if we no longer worship and give offerings to it as in times past, we will always devote it a boundless recognition, admiration and respect.

Aly MAHER EL SAYED
Egyptian Ambassador to France

CONTENTS

THE NILE, BIRTH OF A RIVER

The Sources of the Nile

The Nile: from the heart of Africa to the Mediterranean Sea, the second longest river in the world travels for 4,169 miles through deserts, forests and farming valleys. The sumptuous civilizations fathered and nurtured by the river are fascinating, stupefying, amazing. The unchanging river has witnessed, since the beginning of time, the intrigues of all men called to live with it for a lifetime. On both sides of its banks, for over 5,000 years, successive pharaohs, sultans and presidents have left behind memories of a most glorious past.

Generally, the Nile evokes Egypt, the illustrious land of the pharaohs. However, when it reaches the Sudan-Egyptian border, the river has already travelled more than 78% of its journey to its final destination, the Mediterranean Sea. Where does this imposing tide come from? If one believes the writing of historians, this question had already been raised two thousand years ago by travellers who had vainly attempted to resolve this mystery. For the Egyptians of Antiquity, the question of the sources of the Nile didn't exist. The very idea that the river could come from more distant lands never seems to have been suggested. At least, no Pharaonic text poses such a question. The Nile, was simply an integral element of the universe like any other. From South to North, it winds its harmonious course through Egyptian lands naturally carrying out its role as the providing father. Concerning its sources, popular belief regards the first cataract as both the first place of appearance and point of departure of its interminable voyage towards the north. As for the end of its journey, the Egyptians said that the Nile disappeared into the marshy lands of the delta beyond which nothing existed.

The Greeks and the Romans attributed the Nile to unknown sources, but whose existence would be found at the bottom of a valley in still virgin lands that remained to be discovered. However, the ambition of this project drove the Romans to introduce into their vocabulary an expression that indicated the impossibility of such a mission: *"quaerere fontes Nili"*, *"to seek the sources of the Nile"*, used to denote any project thought to be impossible.

The White Nile

As far back as the fifth century B.C., Greek texts evoked some beliefs handed down from distant oral traditions. *Aeschylus* affirms that the Nile is *"fed by the snows"* and **Herodotus**, in Book Two of *the Histories*, reports the sayings of a scribe of **Sais** who claimed to know the sources of the Nile. *"There are, between Syene, in Thebaid, and Elephantine, two mountains, the name of one is Crophi and the other Mophi. Midway between these two mountains are the fountains of the Nile; half the waters run northward into Egypt, the other half to the South towards Ethiopia."* He concludes with these words: *"One knows that the fountain of the Nile is unfathomable because of an experiment carried out by Psammetichus, an Egyptian King: he sounded the fountain with a rope several thousand fathoms in length but could find no bottom."* A century later, the Greek philosopher **Aristotle** explains to us how the Nile *"descends from a mountain of silver"*. Finally, in the second century A.D., **Claudius Ptolemy**, Greek mathematician, astronomer, and geographer uses all of his scientific rigor in affirming that the origins of the river are the *"Mountains of the Moon whose snows feed the lakes which are the sources of the Nile."* He even points out that the mountains themselves *"rise up at 12°30 latitude and between 57° and 67° longitude"*.

The Valley of the Nile

This map shows the Nile from its sources to the Mediterranean Sea. The Nile is formed by two rivers that join at Khartoum, the capital of Sudan. The White Nile flows from Lake Victoria, at the borders of Tanzania, Kenya and Uganda. After having crossed Lakes Kyoga and Albert, it enters the Sudan through Nimule, across the Sudd, and then flows quietly towards Khartoum. As for the Blue Nile, it has its source in Ethiopia, in Lake Tana. It forms a loop towards the south before heading north-west to reach Khartoum. There the two rivers meet to form only one: The Nile. Its journey through the Sudan, marked by several cataracts, is a little unsteady: it flows due north then turns southward. Finally it arrives in Egypt, pouring into the waters held in Lake Nasser. Passing the Aswan Dam the Nile travels through a valley, surrounded by Libyan and Arabian deserts, which leads it to Cairo where it changes form: it splits into several branches, the two main ones being the Damietta and the Rosetta, to form the Nile Delta. This is the end of its journey for once past the Delta, it flows into the Mediterranean; it has travelled 4,169 miles.

THE NILE VALLEY AND THE MIDDLE-EAST

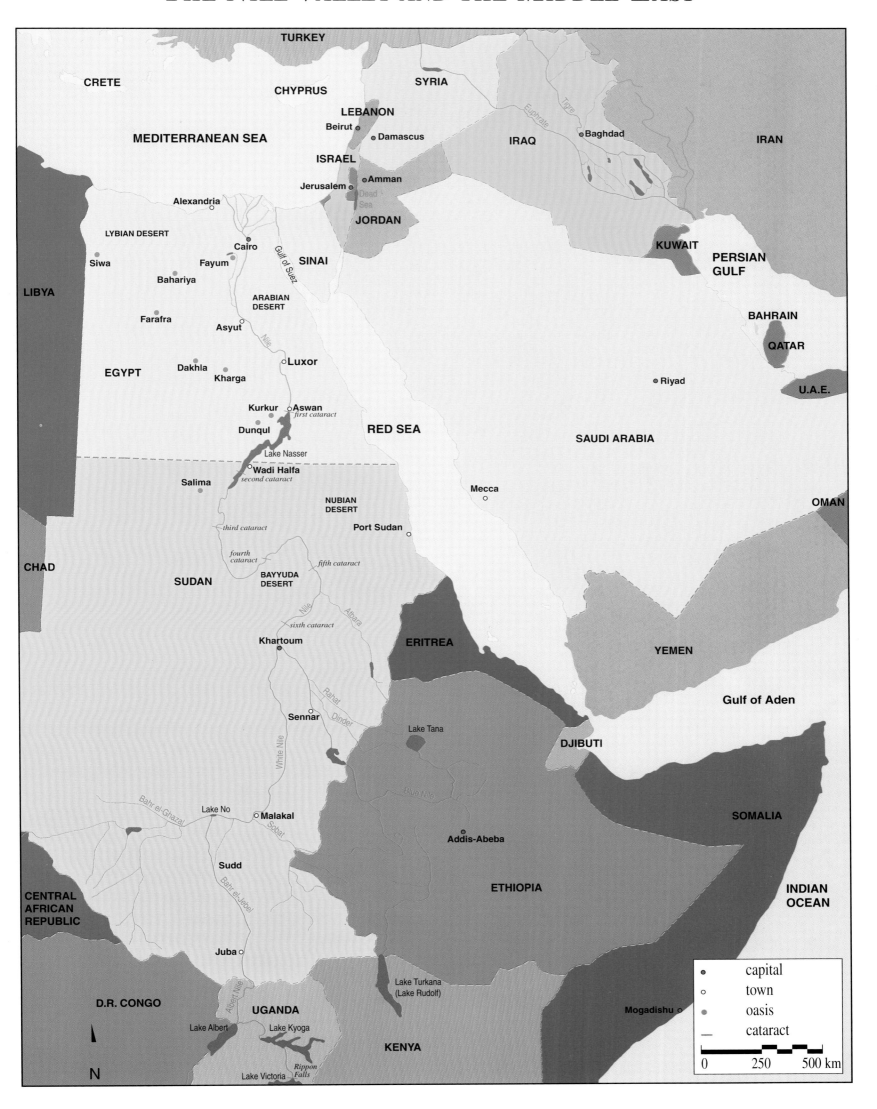

TURKEY

CRETE

CHYPRUS

SYRIA

LEBANON
Beirut
Damascus

MEDITERRANEAN SEA

IRAQ
Baghdad

IRAN

ISRAEL
Jerusalem
Amman
Dead Sea

Alexandria

JORDAN

LYBIAN DESERT

Cairo
Siwa
Fayum
Bahariya

SINAI

Gulf of Suez

KUWAIT

PERSIAN GULF

ARABIAN DESERT

LIBYA

BAHRAIN

QATAR

Farafra
Asyut

Nile

U.A.E.

EGYPT
Dakhla
Kharga
Luxor

Riyad

Kurkur
Aswan
first cataract
Dunqul

RED SEA

SAUDI ARABIA

Lake Nasser

OMAN

Salima
Wadi Halfa
second cataract

Mecca

NUBIAN DESERT

third cataract
Port Sudan

CHAD

fourth cataract
fifth cataract

BAYYUDA DESERT

SUDAN

sixth cataract

YEMEN

Atbara

Nile

Khartoum

ERITREA

Gulf of Aden

Rahat

DJIBUTI

Sennar
Dinder

Lake Tana

White Nile

Bahr el-Ghazal
Lake No
Malakal
Sobat

Blue Nile

SOMALIA

Addis-Abeba

Sudd

Bahr el-Jebel

CENTRAL AFRICAN REPUBLIC

ETHIOPIA

INDIAN OCEAN

Juba

Lake Turkana
(Lake Rudolf)

Albert Nile

D.R. CONGO
UGANDA

Mogadishu

Lake Albert
Lake Kyoga

KENYA

N

Rippon Falls
Lake Victoria

●	capital
○	town
●	oasis
—	cataract

0   250   500 km

The years pass and the nineteenth century lights up with all its fire the valley of the Nile without bringing any additional information to resolve the thorny question of the origins of the great river. It is not that nobody was interested; actually, it was quite on the contrary. But the infrastructure necessary to organise an expedition capable of following the Nile to its source required money, ability and courage. And the unfortunates ones who had already ventured there hardly succeeded in getting past the first indigenous Sudanese and Ugandan tribes or the marshy valleys full of strange animals. Weakened by hunger, exhaustion and sickness, most of them came home empty-handed; some never even returned. However, with each passing voyage, the idea that the Nile came from the great lakes region of Africa became a certainty in people's minds. In the first decades of the century, a certain *Richard Burton*, famous for his numerous expeditions in Africa and Arabia, discovered the **Tanganyika** lake, located on the border between Burundi and Zaïre, which he considered as the providing father of the Nile. This theory, announced with intuition and conviction, but without any real proof, was widely supported. However, nobody of the day was capable of confirming or denying it.

Finally on July 30, 1858, some events begin to take place: *John Hanning Speke*, a young officer from the Indian Army, arrives at **Mwanza**. This small Tanzanian village sits on the Southern coast of a lake of such width that the explorer did not hesitate to conclude that it alone could give birth to such an imposing river like the Nile. Already locally known by the name of **Lake Nyanza**, it fascinated *Speke* who spoke of it in these terms: *"One would call it a sea, a tropical sea, whose banks are overrun by abundant vegetation. This lake is so large that from one bank, one cannot catch a glimpse of the other; it's so long that nobody knows the sheer size of it. It's an immense lake, a lake that's on a scale of the British Empire: that is why I've baptized it Victoria, Victoria Nyanza."*

Astride three countries, Uganda, Tanzania and Kenya, **Lake Victoria**, the second largest lake in the world, covers 42,500 square miles and is nearly one eighth the size of France. With such dimensions, 225 miles long and 156 miles wide, one understands better the term *"interior sea"* used by *Speke* when he revealed his extraordinary find to the members of the Royal Geographical Society in London.

The Tisisat Falls
When the Blue Nile leaves Lake Tana, situated on the high plains of Abyssinia at an altitude of 5,950 feet, the river is calm and serene. This peaceful course, however, is abruptly broken off by the breathtaking Tisisat Falls, which means "steaming water". It falls from a height of 157 feet and covers a width of around 5,600 feet. The Nile is engulfed in a narrow canyon whose walls can reach up to 2,100 feet high, blocking any access to the river, which certainly explains why human inhabitants are rare in this part of Ethiopia.
Tisisat Falls,
Lake Tana region,
Ethiopia.

15

It is in the nineteenth century, the place where British explorers, scholars and geographers gather to confer about their recent research and discoveries carried out to improve the knowledge of the Earth. On this account, the revelations of *Speke* are of utmost importance. But they must be verified: in 1860, *Speke* and *James Augustus Grant*, a colleague from the Indian Army, courageously set off once again for Africa. Two years later, on July 28, 1862, *Speke* reaches, on the north shore of **Lake Victoria**, the very place where the river leaves the immense body of water: these are the high and breathtaking falls which he baptizes the **"Rippon Falls"**.

Reasonably, one could believe that the mystery of the sources of the Nile is finally resolved. Yet one would be mistaken, for over the next fifteen years, three additional expeditions are necessary to confirm this last discovery. In effect, the accidental death of *Speke* and the profound differences of opinion between the partisans of *Burton* and those of *Speke* drive the Royal Geographical Society of London to organise a third journey aimed at definitively resolving the issue. This time, they entrust **Samuel Baker** with the expedition. The information that he brings from Africa does nothing but further obscure the situation more, as in March 1864 he discovers on his route, north-west of **Victoria Nyanza**, Baker discovers a lake of much smaller size that he nonetheless considers the father of the Nile: it appears to be **Lake Albert**. On his return total confusion overcomes the Society: three men and three lakes are at the source of the great river. Which is the right source? *Burton*'s **Lake Tanganyika**, *Speke*'s **Victoria**, or *Baker*'s **Albert**? To answer this question, or to venture an answer, they call upon a trusted man, both a missionary and an explorer. That man is *Livingstone*. Armed with extraordinary courage, he leaves Europe in 1866, determined not to return to London until he has finally resolved between one or another. However, years pass by and England does not receive any news from Africa. The Royal Geographical Society is worried: Is *Livingstone* ill, kept as a prisoner, dead? To resolve this doubt, they send *Stanley*, a journalist from the *New York Herald*, in his search. And *Stanley* finds *Livingstone*. The two get along well, continue their mission and *Stanley* returns to England after having promised his friend to send supplies in order to organise a decisive expedition.

The Tisisat Falls in the Rainy Season

The Nile floods come from the abundance of fallen rain on the mountains of Ethiopia, known by the name of Abyssinia, where the Blue Nile is born. On its route, the river picks up volcanic debris, which gives the Nile its deep brown colour and accounts for its strangely fertile silt. After the rainy season, that ends in late September or early October, the Nile becomes clear again. Gradually its flow decreases until the end of the dry season when the country hardly sees any water.
Tisisat Falls,
Lake Tana region,
Ethiopia.

The porters equipped with provisions take six months to arrive. *Livingstone* sets off en route and reaches **Banguelo**, a small lake situated south of **Lake Tanganyika**. There he thinks he will find a river, the **Lualaba**, which would pour into *Baker*'s **Lake Albert** after having crossed the **Banguelo**. Finally, in 1873 at the end of his treacherous seven-year journey, *Livingstone*, ill and exhausted, dies in **Chitambo**, a village on the banks of **Lake Banguelo**. His death leaves the question in suspense. While a great discouragement takes hold of the British, *Stanley*, a fervent admirer of *Livingstone,* decides to pursue the work of his mentor. For this reason, he sets for Africa in August 1874, and less than two years later provides the definitive solution to the problem: it is **Lake Victoria** which gives birth to the Nile, the White Nile, the "Bahr el-Abiad" of Africans. Fortified by this victory, *Stanley* decides to push his investigations further and, since the Greco-Roman texts speak of mountains feeding the great lakes from which the Nile comes, why not try to locate them more precisely? It is part chance, but also part intuition that allows the explorer to fulfil his vow. Called to Africa to solve a political dispute, *Stanley* avails himself of the opportunity to continually examine Heaven and Earth incessantly in search of the massive mountains. Finally, on May 24, 1888, he finds the famous "*Mountains of the Moon*" of *Claudius Ptolemy*, the **Ruwenzori** of the local population, situated between **Lake Albert** and **Lake Edward**, west of **Victoria Nyanza**. With the conquest of the summit of the **Ruwenzori** by an Italian, their true nature is finally revealed. They are, in point of fact, two mountain peaks with an altitude of more than 17,500 feet and difficult to access as they are shrouded in clouds. From that time on, they were named **Peak Margaret** and **Peak Alexandra**. Thus the epic of the discovery of the White Nile ends. At the beginning of the twentieth century, no mystery remains surrounding the Nile, the lakes, or even the "*Mountains of the moon*". The river can head towards **Khartoum** where it awaits the one who will join it for the rest of its journey to the Mediterranean: the Blue Nile.

The Blue Nile

The discovery of its source goes back to the beginning of the seventeenth century, to 1618 to be precise. Here again, it is part chance that brings *Father Paez*, a Portuguese missionary in Ethiopia, on the route of the Blue Nile. One of his evangelical journeys takes him to the region of **Lake Tana**. There, on the west side of the lake, there is a river known as the **Little Abbai** which heads almost immediately southward under the name of **Great Abbai**; the Blue Nile, that is. Following the river to its source, he quickly discovers the origin of this second Nile: the **Gish Abbai**. Lacking the least techniques to make an exact topographical map and take precise measurements, he contents himself with making a most faithful and true description of the area, carefully noting down to the smallest detail the characteristics of both the source and the surrounding landscape. Of course, such precautions would not be enough to guarantee credit for the discovery from those tempted to seize it at the first opportunity: in 1770, a Scotsman named *Bruce* arrives in Ethiopia, maps the area and returns to Europe four years later determined to reap the benefits of such a remarkable discovery. However, despite some controversy, justice is done: *Father Paez* is recognized as the true discoverer of the Blue Nile.

The Route of Khartoum

Here then are our two twin rivers. One setting out from Uganda and the other from Ethiopia, ready to face many thousands of miles before reaching their meeting point. For the White Nile, it is 1,616 miles to cover, through rich, varied and often incredible African lands. Dams, lakes and rapids follow each other in a disconcerting rhythm, at times forcing the river to surrender its course to the whims of the wild land. At **Murchinson Falls**, in Uganda, the Nile shows what it is capable of. Just before entering *Baker*'s **Lake Albert**, there is a waterfall of more than 140 feet. Its generous waters nourish the luxuriant flora and fauna which thrive in exceptional conditions of heat and humidity. Brilliantly coloured tropical plants, palms and forests burst forth everywhere; elephants, hippopotamuses, giraffes, gorillas, crocodiles, gazelles, flamingos, teeming fish and birds, add their cries and roars to the tumult of the Nile. When the Nile leaves Uganda, the river has travelled about 345 miles, almost 10% of its total journey. The Nile now enters the Sudan by the **Fola** rapids which for many miles force the river to make its way between two narrow cliffs through a narrow canyon.

If one were to ascribe a nationality to the Nile it would certainly be Sudanese. In effect, it crosses the country from south to north, from **Nimule** (starting point of the **Fola** rapids) to **Wadi Halfa**, for a total of 2,406 miles, almost 68.5% of its journey. This situation may strike as paradoxical since it is above all in Egypt where the Nile offers its blessings to man. On the other hand, in Sudan, at least until **Khartoum**, the river keeps to itself through desolate and uninhabited lands preventing anyone from benefiting or exploiting it. This is notably the case of the **Styx**, the name given by *Baker* to the region locally known as the **Sudd**. The name comes from the Arabic *"sadd"*, or "dam". From **Juba** to **Lake No** it is 437.5 miles of marshes or swamps which are almost impenetrable. Explorers frequently mention the whims of the **Sudd**, which gives an ill welcome to all those who dare confront it. Even today there are few who risk it, so perilous is the crossing. Only the few accounts of the most reckless explorers tell of such a journey, and even now it remains quite difficult to get an accurate picture of the **Sudd**. They speak of oversized trees and plants, sometimes reaching dozens of feet in height, thrown together in such wild chaos as to make navigation almost impossible. Besides these constant natural barriers, malaria-bearing mosquitoes inhabit this most inhospitable place. However, in the heart of this swampy jungle, tribes have lived along the banks of the Nile for many generations. They are known as the *Dinka*, and they belong to a group referred to as "Nilotics".

The term "Nilotic" applies to the people living along the valley of the Nile or the native inhabitants. More precisely, it refers to people whose culture and language belong to those of *Shilluk*, *Nuer* and the *Dinka*. These are the first people to have been qualified as "Nilotic", because, contrary to certain groups established in areas largely outside the boundaries of the valley of the Nile, they really dwell in the valley of the White Nile. Like the majority of Nilotics, the *Dinka* are of great height, slim, with long and thinly muscled limbs, and their physique is similar to that of Europeans. They shave their heads, which at times they decorate with a feathered head clothing, and generally wander around naked, armed with a javelin or club. Anthropologists refer to them as "Birdmen". As a matter of fact, they are in the habit of standing on one leg, the other one being tucked away flamingo-like, and of walking in immense strides, slow and slender rather like storks. The bulk of their diet comes from seed, corn and vegetables, but their regard for the practice of agriculture is somehow rather moderate. On the other hand, they have quite an incredible passion for the rearing of livestock in general and cows in particular; a passion that for some of them can become a genuine reason to live. Traditionally, and particularly with the *Dinka*, cows are not eaten. This is a rule that can be violated only when the cow has died accidentally or of old age, and especially when its meat is still edible, an exceptional thing with old beasts. The cow dominates and directs the social life of an entire Dinka tribe. Most of the time these are beautiful animals and it is not surprising the care being lavished on them. Judging by the accounts of the explorers who spent time with one or another of these tribes, to possess a cow is to live; to lose it, to die somehow. Certain texts explain how the owner of a deceased cow is capable of sinking into a profound lethargy for several days; there is nothing anyone can do to console him, so great is his grief. Occasionally, the very idea of surviving a beloved animal can be too much to bear and can even lead to suicide.

The Nile reaches the end of its crossing of the **Styx** when it pours into **Lake No**: we are now 594 miles from **Khartoum**. Over the course of this long and difficult journey the level of the river diminishes considerably. This is certainly due to plain evaporation, but also because of the overabundant vegetation and the enormous quantities of water it consumes. Fortunately, the **Bahr el-Zaraf** and the **Sobat** come to the rescue, supplying water and fertile silt. When it flows into the Nile, 75 miles from **Lake No,** the **Sobat** arrives directly from the high plains of Ethiopia. Not only does it add its load of volcanic debris; more importantly, it doubles the size of the river which in this way recovers all the water lost during the crossing of the **Styx**. The last outstanding stage before the meeting of the two Niles is **Kosti**, 178 miles from **Khartoum**. This town deserves to be mentioned because it marks the frontier between two very different zones of the Sudan. To the south there is nothing but virgin forests and marshes inhabited by the Nile people.

To the north, the exuberant vegetation disappears, yielding to the desert; and the *Dinka*, the *Shilluk* and the *Nuer* give way to the Muslim population. From this point on, the Nile adopts the character it will retain until it reaches the Mediterranean Sea: the river in the centre, the palm groves and crops on either bank. And the desert beyond, as far as the eye can see.

In this way the White Nile can cover the last few dozen of miles which still separate it from **Khartoum** where, right on time, its Siamese twin awaits, the Blue Nile. But what has it done since **Gish Abbai**, its point of departure? It has travelled over 977 miles, approximately 625 miles less than the White Nile, and those in a different way. What is commonly known as the Blue Nile is in fact a river which simultaneously possesses three different names depending where it is: the **Little Abbai** (from **Gish Abbai** to **Lake Tana**), the **Great Abbai** (from **Lake Tana** to **Roseires**) and finally **Bahr el-Azrak** (from **Roseires** to **Khartoum**). Paradoxically, it is a small river which slips from **Gish Abbai**: small but resolute. Taking the direction to **Lake Tana**, it attracts with a sly magnetism the surrounding waters which rapidly turn this modest river into a great current; it is this river which flows into **Lake Tana** from the west and then, strangely, leaves at the furthermost southern point. The new direction becomes even more surprising: it travels towards the south-east while **Khartoum** is in the exact opposite direction, that is, to the north-west. This is certainly nothing more than a whim, but it forces the Nile to make a long loop before resetting its course for the Sudan.

One of the most important characteristics of the Blue Nile is its power, acquired thanks to the very uneven terrain it crosses. Until **Bumbodi**, a frontier town between Ethiopia and Sudan, it descends an average of 8.5 feet per mile. This difference in height, considered of great benefit, gives the river the tremendous force which allows it to carry everything it finds along with it, especially the famous silt, product of the erosion of volcanic rocks in the Ethiopian mountains. It is this silt which has for millennia assured the subsistence of the inhabitants of the Nile Valley. However, if in Egypt the Nile is synonymous of fertility and abundance, in Ethiopia things are quite different. In this country, the Nile often flows in deep inaccessible gorges, obliging men to live on the arid plateau, far from its waters and its silt.

**Bahar Dar,
to the Source of the
Blue Nile**
From the start, the Blue Nile is little more than a modest river, called Little Abbai. It flows into Lake Tana from the west and leaves from the south by the name Great Abbai, that is, the Blue Nile. Bahar Dar, the most important village of the entire region is located on the very spot where the Blue Nile flows out of the lake. It is here that the indigenous inhabitants come regularly to sell their wood. They come in boats made of papyrus or woven reeds and travel for up to eight hours to reach Bahar Dar. The Nile is very calm in this place; like the lake, it is perfectly navigable. However, the calm is an uneasy one, for the Tisisat Falls are very near, preventing the exploitation of the area as a transportation route.
Bahar Dar, Lake Tana region, Ethiopia.

After **Bumbodi**, the Nile becomes calm. Serenely, it covers the remaining 456 miles, still conserving enough force to carry its riches and deposits to **Khartoum**. After the **Roseires** dam, close to a hydroelectric power station, the Nile becomes navigable, a remarkable fact, given the power of the Blue Nile. It arrives in **Sennar** which in Sudan symbolizes the gates of paradise. Beyond stretches **Gezira**, the granary of the country. Over almost 2.47 million acres, all kinds of cereals and cotton are cultivated at a great profit. It must be added that here the Nile is enriched yet again by two rivers that also carry the rich silt: the **Dinder** and the **Rahat**.

The city of **Khartoum** finally comes into view; this is where the White Nile in the west and the Blue Nile in the east join to form the one and only Nile. Its first objective is to cross the Sudan to get to Egypt. For this task it does not take the most direct route. Through the desert, the river takes a long, tortuous, S-shaped route, and almost seems to return to the south by mistake. Six cataracts punctuate its course, marked by rapids with islands, islets and massive massifs at times several miles long. Paradoxically, they are numbered in the inverse of the course of the Nile; the sixth cataract is the first one reached after leaving **Khartoum**. These cataracts are often mentioned, not only for their own particular interest but especially because they are excellent landmarks in a somewhat abandoned region.

Naga

Situated upriver from the sixth cataract and far from the Nile, Naga remains one of the most beautiful sites of the Meroitic period. Many temples are still visible, particularly this small pavilion erected between the second and third centuries A.D. It is a hybrid composition, fusing Egyptian, Greek and Roman traditions. Notably one can see on the lintel above the main entrance a frieze of cobras symbolizing the uraeus of the pharaohs. Below appears Ra, the sun god, protected by two vulture wings. These images are both typically Egyptian. On the other hand, the structure of the temple, with its vaults, its columned walls and sculpted capitals, is of Greco-Roman origin.
Pavilion of Naga,
Meroitic era,
Naga, Sudan.

Nubia

We are now in the land of the ancient Egyptians: **Kush**; the land historians call Nubia (from the hieroglyph "*noub*", or gold). From the beginning of the Pharaonic era, Egypt seeks to take hold of this fabulous source of raw materials: its sway reaches the first cataract during the Archaic era and the second cataract at the time of the First dynasty, under the rule of the king *Djer*. During the Middle Kingdom, *Senusret III* subdues Nubia all the way to **Semneh**, upriver from the second cataract. He devises a system of fortifications to seal the frontier in order to control the movements of the Nubian population and the traffic on the river. With the New Kingdom, a real political administration develops. The pharaoh, who henceforth would control the country up to the fourth cataract, entrusts the rule of this domain to a high Theban administrator, "the Royal Son of **Kush**", assisted by two lieutenants. Mercenaries, slaves, workers, gold, ivory and livestock are all directly imported from Nubia. But "the Royal Son of **Kush**" also deals with sending a whole range of products from more distant African lands to Egypt: perfumes, rare essences, embroidered textiles, precious stones, rare woods, wild animals… By the second millennium B.C., Egyptian ascendancy is such that the Nubians end up adopting hieroglyphic writing, as well as the customs and divinities directly taken from Pharonic traditions. Nubia is covered with many finely crafted temples, the most interesting of which were removed to Upper Egypt at the time of the construction of the **Aswan** Dam.

However, by the end of the Ramesses era, during the Third Middle Period, Egypt is engulfed by a political and social upheaval; the land of **Kush** takes advantage of the turmoil to seize its independence. The Nubians found an independent kingdom, centred in **Napata**, downriver from the fourth cataract; from there they embark upon the conquest of Egypt. *Piy*, ruler of the Nubian kingdom, swiftly reaches **Thebes**, conquers Lower Egypt and takes power; in this way the 25th Dynasty, the so called "Ethiopian" or Kushite is established. For more than sixty years, five pharaohs succeed to the throne of Egypt. However, the last one, *Tanutamani*, pursued by the Assyrians in 664 B.C., flees the valley of the Nile and finds refuge in **Napata**.

Shortly afterwards, the decline and abandonment of the capital, due to new political, economic and strategic considerations, obliges the king of **Napata** to move further south. He chooses a much more fertile area to the north of the sixth cataract as the centre of the new kingdom; a site which is 162 miles from modern day **Khartoum**: **Meroe**. In this way the second Ethiopian kingdom is born; directly stemming from the previous **Napata** kingdom. Power and creativity characterize this new civilization: a combination of elements gathered from many different African cultures and from Hellenistic traditions. From the valley of the Nile the Thebaide triad (*Amun, Mut* and *Khons*) and the guardian divinities of beyond (*Isis, Osiris, Nephthys* and *Anubis*) were taken; at the same time, local gods, particularly the lion *Apedemak*, retained an important place in the Meroitic pantheon.

The new sanctuaries boast strange reliefs whose scenes and characters possess a number of characteristics taken from Pharaonic Egypt (postures), the first Ethiopian kingdom of **Napata** (the ram of *Amun* and the double **uraeus**) and from local traditions (voluptuous bodies heavily ornamented with complicated finery). Slowly, the Nubian capital declines. The population abandons the town and **Meroe** finally dies out at the dawn of the fourth century A.D., giving way to the Christians and later to the Muslims.

The area occupied by ancient Nubia begins at **Khartoum** and ends in Egyptian territory, around **Aswan**. It is divided into two distinct regions: Upper Nubia, from **Khartoum** to **Wadi Halfa**, which marks the actual frontier between Sudan and Egypt; and Lower Nubia, from **Wadi Halfa** to **Aswan**. In Upper Nubia, the Nile travels about 940 miles during which it makes two great curves: at first, it changes course and heads resolutely towards the south-west, then, it recovers its initial direction and takes its route northwards. When it leaves **Khartoum**, the river quickly finds itself confronted by the churning eddies of the sixth cataract. On the banks of the river, lie the last vestiges of two sacred towns. The first, **Naga**, is one of the most beautiful sites known of the Meroitic era. It was built by King *Natakamani* and Queen *Amanitore* in the first century A.D. and displays a subtle mixture of styles: Egyptian, Greco-Roman and Nubian. The second, **Mussawarat** is remarkable for its immense size: an enclosure with a perimeter of 4,200 feet surrounds necropoleis and sanctuaries, the oldest of which date back to the fifth century B.C. Both possess a temple dedicated to the lion *Apedemak*, the dominant divinity of the Meroitic pantheon, along with *Amun*, the Egyptian God of the Empire. On his own, *Apedemak* symbolises life and fertility, strength and power, cosmic order and equilibrium in the world. In the majority of representations, he is depicted either as a warrior god dressed as a soldier and striking his enemies or as a providing god carrying a bushel of sorghum and adorned with the cross of life.

Some miles north of **Mussawarat** lies the ancient city of **Meroe**, the second capital of the Nubian kingdom. The name **Meroe** applies both to the city and to the remarkable civilization which developed from **Aswan** to **Khartoum** between the sixth century B.C. to the third century A.D. Surrounded by a defensive wall, the royal city is found near the Nile. Besides the sanctuaries, the audience halls, the astronomic observatories and the baths, archaeologists have discovered astonishing quantities of slag resulting from iron works, an activity which certainly added to the prosperity of **Meroe**. Outside the city, there stand diverse religious buildings, notably the Temple of the Sun which, according to *Heliodorus*, would have been used during military parades. However, for the visitor, **Meroe**'s interest lies particularly in the discovery of its three necropoleis, situated on small hills in the open desert, quite far to the east.

The southern necropolis, called royal but being only partially so, has more than two hundred tombs belonging to kings, queens and members of noble families who, after the reign of *Piy*, resided in **Meroe**. The tombs have diverse forms: they are long steeply terraced pyramids of sandstone, **mastabas** or simply excavated vaults. From 250 B.C., the necropolis became useless due to lack of space. Therefore the rulers chose another hill further north to serve as a burial ground. As opposed to the southern necropolis, this one is purely royal; it holds the bodies of the kings, queens and crown princes of **Meroe** from the middle of the third century B.C. to the fourth century A.D.

One finds three types of pyramids: the first are identical to the ones found in the southern necropolis; the second ones are characterised by smooth angled faces and funerary chambers, generally grouped in threesomes and covered with scenes taken from the Egyptian "**Book of the Dead**"; the last type of pyramids are much less rich since under the terraced sandstone surface there appears a mass of loose stones rather than matching blocks. Then, there is left the western necropolis which was used by high officials and notables of the kingdom. There are around five hundred tombs of which a hundred are pyramids. Nearly all of them are built on the same model: a funeral chapel, sometimes closed by a door or a pylon; a vault located under the pyramid and accessible through a shaft.

Having crossed the region of **Atbara**, a region renowned for its very rich citrus orchards and produce, the Nile reaches the fifth cataract. Not far from there a rocky mass covered in writings, known by the name of **Hagar el-Merwa**, marks the official limit of the Egyptian New Kingdom. Once past the cataract, the river follows its course until **Abu Hamed** where it quickly forks to the south to reach the fourth cataract.

The Lion of Apedemak
Apedemak is one of the main gods of the Meroitic pantheon. It symbolises fertility, cosmic order and equilibrium in the universe. In presiding over combat, he brandishes a standard and wears a coat of mail. Very often, the Meroitic towns of the south boast amung their ruins a temple dedicated to Apedemak. Such is the case with Naga: the temple dates from the time of King Natakamani and Queen Amanitare who reigned around the first century A.D. Like all the cult buildings of the town, it combines both Egyptian and Greco-Roman characteristics.
Temple of Apedemak,
Meroitic era,
Naga, Sudan.

There are some 94 miles of rocky obstacles to be crossed before reaching the heart of the **Bayuda** desert. This desolate region is nearly inaccessible due to the lack of suitable roads and the impossibility of following the river especially during times of low water.

The Nile then gets to the kingdom of **Napata**, installed at the foot of the sacred mountain of **Gebel Barkal**. From a height of 340 feet, this mountain dominates the surrounding plains. Founded by the Egyptian pharaohs of the 18th Dynasty, the city of **Napata** very quickly became, because of its location at the place where the Nile changes course, a strategic point of primary importance and very likely, a flourishing market for products from the rest of Africa as a centre for gold exchange. However, from the end of the Ramesses era, new demands forced Egypt to veer towards the Mediterranean Sea: Nubia is then abandoned and sinks into obscurity. For more than two hundred years up until the beginning of the ninth century B.C., historians are confronted by a surprising historical void. It is barely known that an indigenous dynasty from **el-Kurru**, a small town south of **Napata**, begins to become more and more powerful and contemplates a conquest of Egypt. The famous "**Stele of Victory**" of *Piy*, written in 715 B.C., recalls the formidable Nubian invasion of the land of the pharaohs. Under his successor, *Shabaqo*, the Nubian kings take control of the Nile Valley and found the 25th Dynasty. **Napata** becomes the capital of an immense kingdom extending from the Mediterranean Sea to the fourth cataract. Afterwards, despite the conquest of Egypt by the Assyrians and the foundation of the **Meroe** kingdom, the city retains its role as a religious centre thanks to the protection it enjoys of **Gebel Barkal**, the sacred mountain. At its foot lie the vestiges of a civilization strongly marked by Egyptian influences. The main temple is dedicated to the god *Amun*; a second, much smaller one, is reserved for the cult of the goddess *Mut*. Both adopt the construction style of Pharaonic temples: **dromos**, pylons, great peristyle courts, hypostyle rooms and sacred chapels.

Recent archaeological excavations have permitted the discovery of a building, certainly related to the temple of *Amun*, which has been identified as an imposing royal palace built for the king *Natakamani* after the sacking of the town by the Roman armies of *Petronius*. Nearby is the necropolis of **el-Kurru**, composed of the tombs of the first kings of **Napata** and the pyramids of *Piy*, *Shabaqo*,

Shabitqo and *Tanutamani*, along with the tombs of their queens, buried in places especially reserved for them. Concerned about the lack of space and wishing to reproduce the Theban model, *Taharqo* decided to inaugurate a new site, **Nuri**, located on the left bank of the river; thus, the tombs of **Gebel Barkal** would be a replica of **Karnak** and the necropolis of **Nuri**, that of the **Valley of the Kings**. From *Taharqo* on, until 300 B.C., all the kings, except for *Tanutamani*, have a tomb here despite the fact that the capital was moved to **Meroe** two centuries before. All the pyramids, of which the most imposing is that of *Taharqo*, with sides measuring 98 feet (the sides of the *Khufu* pyramid measures 805 feet at the base), consist of narrow sandstone terraces, usually with two or three subterranean chambers.

Between the fourth and third cataracts the Nile forms a loop which allows it to retake its course northwards.

To reach the **Dongola** basin, administrative centre of the region, the river crosses well irrigated land, where palm groves particularly abound. On the right bank of the river stand the remains of **Dongola el-Aguz**, capital of the Christian kingdom of **Makuria**. The origin of Christian kingdoms date back to the sixth century. Byzantine monks, eager to convert to Christianity the populations located to the south of Egypt, entered Nubia and founded three kingdoms between the present day towns of **Aswan** and **Khartoum**: **Alodia** in the south, **Makuria** in the centre, and **Nobatia** in the north. In the seventh century, the kingdoms of **Makuria** and **Nobatia** join together in order to better resist the Arab conquerors. During almost eight centuries, the Muslims of Egypt and the Christians of Nubia live together without too much conflict; but the rules are clear: the Nubians must pay an annual tribute to the Egyptian governor. However the Arab armies end up invading the Nubian territory and,

little by little, the Christian kingdoms lose their independence; by the sixteenth century Nubia is Islamised.

At **Dongola el-Aguz** some vestiges still remain of the kingdom's grandeur. On a little hill, the royal palace, converted into a mosque in 1317, dominates an area of domed tombs built in the middle of the desert. Along the length of the river, remain the ruins of different buildings of the ancient Christian city: cathedrals, basilicas and monasteries which were excavated by a Polish mission over more than thirty years.

The Nile then enters the royal kingdom of **Kush**, whose capital **Kerma** is situated on the right bank up-river from the third cataract. This brilliant civilization, contemporary of the Egyptian Middle Kingdom, appeared in 2400 B.C. and declined some nine hundred years later with the conquest of Nubia by the pharaohs of the 18th Dynasty. Its prosperity essentially depended on its commercial activities.

Temple of Apedemak

Throughout the whole of the Meroitic era and along with Mussawarat, Naga played the role of Meroe's sacred city, the capital of the Nubia kingdom. Both have temples dedicated to the Lion of Apedemak, main divinity of the Nubian pantheon. That of Naga, built in the first century A.D., is remarkable for its state of preservation. If one believes researchers, it was modelled after the Horus-dedicated Temple of Edfu; its exterior appearance, its layout, and its architectural lines are in fact identical to the latter's. Only the images, mainly dedicated to the Nubian gods and to Apedemak, differ.
Temple of Apedemak
Meroitic era,
Naga, Sudan.

27

The kingdom is not only established in the rich and fertile agricultural basin but, in addition, it controls the trade routes which lead to the Mediterranean Sea and to the Red Sea. Exotic products and precious materials from Africa pass through here. The fortified city of **Kerma** contains an important religious quarter dominated by the **"deffufa"**, the largest temple in the city. It looks like an enormous mass of brick 63 feet high and 182 feet long. On both sides there are chapels, stores, annexes, bakeries, and workshops to serve the needs of the cult. Further south an area extends that could have been the royal residence: a great hut, some 58 feet in diameter, no doubt an audience hall or meeting room, shares the space devoted to dwellings and stores. Many necropoleis have been uncovered which give a very precise insight into the rites that accompanied the funerals and the type of funerary items that were put into the tombs. For example, it has been found that, in the princely tombs of classical **Kerma** (between 1750 and 1500 B.C.), burial mounds of some 350 feet in diameter at least, the sovereign was accompanied by hundreds of human sacrifices, three or four hundred in some cases, and abundant funerary objects: tools, clothes, furniture, ceramics, woven baskets, weapons…

Just before reaching the third cataract, the Nile arrives at the granite rocks of **Tombos** which mark the furthest advance of the pharaonic armies at the beginning of the New Kingdom. Indeed, after victoriously reaching the cataract, *Thutmose I* fixes the new Egyptian frontier at this point and declares it will never be violated by the Nubians. The words, carved into the rocks, mention the presence of a fortress built to prevent any Nubian incursions but it has not yet been located by archaeologists. Past the cataract, the Nile continues its voyage along the Arab-era castles which dot the **"Sesebi** passage", and reaches **Soleb**. There, on the west bank, stands a magnificent temple of Nubian sandstone built for *Amenhotep III* by the architect of **Luxor**, *Amenhotep son of Hapu*. It is dedicated to two divinities: *Amun-Ra* of **Karnak** and *Nebmaatra*, Lord of Nubia, the divine form of *Amenhotep III*, associated with the lunar god *Khons*. The Pharaoh appears in the guise of a man with a divine loincloth, wearing the **nemes** and his ear covered with a ram horn, the sacred animal of *Amun*; on his head he wears a crescent moon and a solar disk. The scene carved

on the walls relate to the king's first jubilee and to the rites necessary in preparation for this important occasion. The ritual of the "Illumination of the Thrones" invokes *Nebmaatra* so as to ensure the regular appearance of the moon and the healing eye of *Horus*.

In fact, many Egyptian myths refer to the flight of the eye to Nubia and its struggle against the enemies of *Ra*. Appeased, the god gives the full moon and its return to Egypt brings abundance and prosperity. Generally, this eye takes the form of the lion goddess *Tefenet-Mehit*, which can be translated as "the fullness of the moon". It is very probable that the two lions in rose granite discovered at **Gebel Barkal** and preserved in the **British Museum** come from **Soleb** and exactly represent this calm and appeased lioness. A few miles north of **Soleb** lie the ruins of the small temple of **Sedeinga**, consecrated to *Tiy*, the Great Royal Spouse of *Amenhotep III*. Here, the queen incarnates the vengeful aspect of the eye of the sun who has left Egypt to seek refuge in Nubia. As in **Soleb**, the rites practised in the temple certainly aim to appease the terrible lioness and to ask her to adopt the peaceful character of the goddess *Hathor*. Unfortunately, the majestic "dwelling of *Tiy*" is today reduced to a pile of fallen stones from which a single column emerges with a hathoric capital, that is, decorated on its four sides with a humanised figure of the cow *Hathor*.

The Nile reaches the last straight line that separates it from **Lake Nasser**. A little past **Sedeinga**, it comes to the **island of Sai**. Vestiges of the entire history of Nubia from prehistory to the Arab era can be found on this island: necropoleis, buildings of the Egyptian New Kingdom, Christian churches, Ottoman fortresses…

Amara appears astride the river; here, to the east, there is a Meroitic temple; to the west, a temple dedicated to *Ramesses II*. Finally the river arrives at **Aksha** where it flows into the artificial lake. Before the **Aswan** dam was built, this is where the second cataract, called the "Throat of Stone", the **Batn el-Haggar**, an arid and pitiless desert whose 50-miles length formed an almost impassable barrier, were to be found. The nine fortresses, each of them protected by three enclosures built by the pharaohs of the Middle Kingdom to protect against Nubian incursions, now sleep peacefully beneath the waters of **Lake Nasser**. It is here that the Nile prepares to leave the Sudan and enter the land of Egypt.

**Meroe,
a "Forest" of Pyramids**

Meroe played the role of capital of the Nubian kingdom from the fourth century B.C. to the fourth A.D. The city is located on the banks of the Nile, north of the two sacred cities, Naga and Mussawarat. It has three necropoleis which, amung the hundreds of tombs, includes two hundred pyramids. It is by far the most beautiful funerary group in the Sudan: certain pyramids are still very well preserved.
Necropolis of Meroe,
Meroitic era,
Meroe, Sudan.

Nubia saved from the waters

**Abu Simbel,
an Exemplary Salvation**

*The moving of the temple of
Ramesses II at Abu Simbel is the
shining success story of the
Unesco-run campaign to save
the Nubian temples. It was carried 224 feet from its original
site, to prevent its disappearance beneath the waters of
Lake Nasser. Nearly nine hundred people, from diverse fields,
worked for five years to return
Abu Simbel to its original state.*
Temple of Ramesses II,
New Kingdom,
Abu Simbel, Upper Egypt.

The construction of the **Aswan** dam has meant
the total disappearance of the region immediately
upriver, Lower Nubia. It has been inundated, engulfed
and condemned by **Lake Nasser**, an immense reservoir
measuring no less than 312 miles long by 6.5 to
18.5 miles wide. Populations and archaeological remains
have had to be moved. One seldom recalls the evacuation
of the Nubian population. Yet close to eighty
thousand people were forced to abandon their homes
and native villages for austere, inhospitable and
unknown lands. Nubians and Ethiopians left for the
south in search of a land that would welcome them,
while the Egyptians took the route to Upper Egypt,
moving to the regions of **Kom Ombo**, **Esna**, **Edfu**,
or even **Gebel el-Silsila**, one of the most arid zones in
the country.

On the other hand, what was most eagerly talked
about was the great project to save the monuments of
Lower Nubia. It must be recognized that the work performed is fantastic, lacking neither originality, nor courage, nor ability. The campaign for the "Salvation of the
Sites and Monuments of Nubia" was inaugurated on
March 8, 1960, by Unesco. That day, *Vittorio Veronese*
launched an appeal to world solidarity for the salvation
of the Nubian patrimony. The operation consisted of two
parts: increase the surveys and archaeological search of
the area bound to disappearance, and dismantle the principal structures in order to move them to locations safe
from the waters. The message met with a warm recep-
tion as teams from all over the world, made up of scientists from diverse fields, worked successfully in this
enormous enterprise. However, only certain monuments
from the Pharaonic era profited from the dismantling and
reconstruction project.

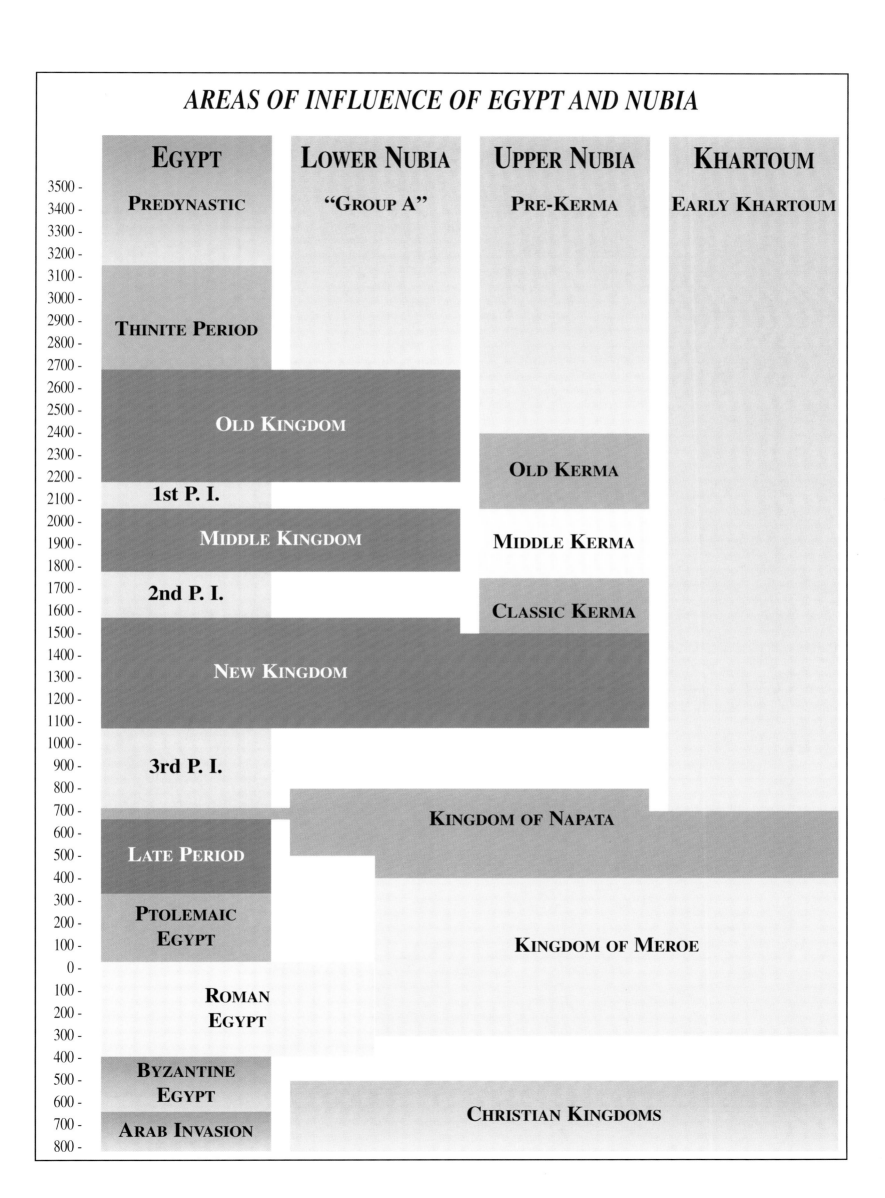

AREAS OF INFLUENCE OF EGYPT AND NUBIA

EGYPT	LOWER NUBIA	UPPER NUBIA	KHARTOUM
PREDYNASTIC	"GROUP A"	PRE-KERMA	EARLY KHARTOUM

3500 -
3400 -
3300 -
3200 -
3100 -
3000 -
2900 -
2800 - THINITE PERIOD
2700 -
2600 -
2500 -
2400 - OLD KINGDOM
2300 - OLD KERMA
2200 -
2100 - 1st P. I.
2000 -
1900 - MIDDLE KINGDOM   MIDDLE KERMA
1800 -
1700 - 2nd P. I.
1600 - CLASSIC KERMA
1500 -
1400 -
1300 - NEW KINGDOM
1200 -
1100 -
1000 -
900 - 3rd P. I.
800 -
700 - KINGDOM OF NAPATA
600 -
500 - LATE PERIOD
400 -
300 -
200 - PTOLEMAIC
100 - EGYPT
0 -
100 - KINGDOM OF MEROE
200 - ROMAN
300 - EGYPT
400 -
500 - BYZANTINE
600 - EGYPT
700 - CHRISTIAN KINGDOMS
800 - ARAB INVASION

**The Temple of
Abu Simbel**

*The Abu Simbel site consists of
two cave temples (called speos)
of the 19th Dynasty. The two buildings date from the reign of
Ramesses II: the first is dedicated
to Ra-Harakhty, to Amun and to
the deified king; the second one,
to Hathor and to queen Nefertari.
The temple façade consists of
four colossal statues of Ramesses
II, 70 feet high. Pharaoh is sitting
with his hands poised on his
knees. His forehead is ornamented with royal uraeus, his head is
covered with the nemes and he is
wearing the kings' false beard.
This temple, carved out of a cliff,
is one of the most beautiful buildings in the Nile Valley.*
Temple of Ramesses II,
New Kingdom,
Abu Simbel, Upper Egypt.

All the other constructions, nearly three hundred according to *Jean Vercoutter*, director of the **Khartoum Antiquities Service** at the time of the construction of the dam, have disappeared beneath the waters of the lake. Some of the temples saved by the international community have been regrouped in four areas situated along the western bank of **Lake Nasser** (**Abu Simbel**, **Amada**, **Wadi es-Sebua** and **Kalabsha**), others have been gene-rously donated to foreign countries, in gratitude for their cooperation.

Some miles from the Sudan border, 170 miles south of **Aswan**, stand the temples of **Abu Simbel**, the reconstruction of which has to be considered as the symbol of the salvation campaign organized by Unesco. The site consists of two **speos** built under the reign of *Ramesses II*: the first is dedicated to *Ra-Harakhty*, *Amun* and *Ramesses II*, the second to *Hathor* and queen *Nefertari*. To move the two structures 224 feet from

their original location, workers from fifty countries totalling around nine hundred people worked without respite for five years in order to return the Ramesses's temples to their original condition. The works began in 1963 while the construction of the "high dam" was already under way and the water had begun to tickle the colossal feet of the majestic *Ramesses*. Before anything, it was necessary to build a dike large enough to be able to contain the rising waters. At the same time, the temples were separated from the cliff: more than 65,000 tons of debris were thus removed. With these two opera-tions completed, the technicians proceeded with the cutting of the twin temples into more than a thousand pieces. This work was all the more delicate as the sand-stone was very fragile; utmost care had to be taken to specifically avoid the random breaking which would risk damaging the aesthetics of the monuments once they were reassembled. Once removed, each block was carefully numbered and stacked. On the newly chosen

location, a gigantic concrete superstructure was erected to support the entire edifice. Everything was eventually ready for reassembly: one by one, the blocks assumed their places in the heart of the temple. Once the operation was achieved, there remained only to reconstruct the original surroundings: enormous concrete vaults were made, designed to receive the rocky facing similar in size and appearance to that which originally surrounded the two **speos**. Thus, on September 22, 1968, before hundreds of journalists, the Egyptian government inaugurated the new site of **Abu Simbel**. Everything was put back exactly as the architects of *Ramesses II* had conceived and imagined. This great project once and for all demonstrated that the alliance between archaeology and technology had without a doubt a bright future.

Further north, on the right bank of the Nile, there stood the small cave chapel of **el-Lessiya**, created during the reign of *Thutmose III*, of the 18th Dynasty. Offered

to Italy in 1966, it was installed in the **Egyptian Museum of Turin**. This temple is composed of a single recessed room which in the past proceeded from a covered courtyard. The reliefs show the Pharaoh worshipping several divinities, in particular the Nubian god *Dedoun* and the deified *Senusret III*. Originally, the niche contained a group of statues showing *Thutmose III* around *Horus of Mi'am*, the ancient city of **Aniba**, and *Satis*. Damaged during the Amarnian era, it was restored and transformed by *Ramesses II* who had himself depicted between *Amun-Ra* and *Horus of Mi'am*.

The second group of buildings are found 112 miles south of **Aswan**, on the west bank of the lake: the temples of **Amada** and **Derr** as well as the tomb of *Penniut*. The construction of the small temple of **Amada**, consecrated to the gods *Ra-Harakhty* and *Amun-Ra* dates back to *Thutmose III* and *Amenhotep II*. *Thutmose IV* added a hypostyle room, and *Sethos I*, a pylon, of which only a door remains. At the time of the Unesco campaign, the temple of **Amada** received particular attention. Specialists, judging that a traditional disassembly would pose a fatal risk due to the fragility of its reliefs, simply decided to transport it in one piece; it measures 31.5 feet wide by 77 feet long and weighs around 2,000 tons. This operation, undertaken by France, consisted in encasing the building with steel and concrete, placing it on a specially constructed railway and moving it a distance of 9,100 feet to an increased height of 230 feet. By its side stands the cave temple of **Derr.** Originally situated on the right bank of the river Nile, seven miles south of its present site, its transfer was organised by the Egyptian Antiquities Service. It is the "Temple of *Ramesses*, beloved of *Amun* in the Domain of *Ra*", constructed during the second half of *Ramesses II* reign, and identical in design to the great temple of **Abu Simbel**. In the same way, the **speos** is composed of a hypostyle room, a vestibule and a temple at the back of which stand side by side *Ra-Harakhty*, *Ramesses II*, *Amun-Ra* and *Ptah*. This leaves the tomb of *Penniut*, governor of **Wawat** (Lower Nubia) under *Ramesses VI*, which was moved due to the excellent state of preservation of its reliefs. It comes from **Aniba**, a town located 25 miles south of its new emplacement. Its disassembly and reassembly was financed with American capital and executed by the Egyptian Antiquities Service.

On the Banks of Lake Nasser

Lake Nasser is an enormous reservoir formed by the Aswan dam. Situated on the border of Egypt and Sudan, it flooded a region known as Lower-Nubia (from Aswan to Aksha, near the second cataract). On its site, the remains of numerous Pharaonic and Nubian civilizations were found, the most important of which were saved from the waters by the rescue campaign inaugurated by Unesco in 1960. Of the temples which benefited from the operation, some stand on the banks of Lake Nasser, others are in museums. A short four day cruise allows the exploration of the temples along the shores of the lake. Starting from Aswan and arriving at Abu Simbel, the cruise stops at the new sites of Kalabsha, Wadi es-Sebua and Amada, each of which boast many temples.
Temple of Maharraqa,
Greco-Roman era,
Lake Nasser, Upper Egypt.

Moving 25 miles north, the new site of **Wadi es-Sebua** is home to a temple of *Ramesses II*, the hypostyle room of **Maharraqa** and the temple of **Dakka**, all three buildings reconstructed by the Egyptian Antiquities Service. The "Temple of *Ramesses*, beloved of *Amun*, in the Domain of *Amun*" is a construction which today is better known nowadays as **Wadi es-Sebua**, the "Valley of the Lions", in reference to the sphinx **dromos** which precedes the temple entrance. It is a building erected between the 35th and 50th year of the reign of *Ramesses II* in honour of *Ra-Harmakhis* and *Amun-Ra*. Moved 2.5 miles to the north-east of the ancient site, the temple consists of an unroofed area, the pylon and the portico-lined courtyard, a part dug into the mountain, the vestibule opening onto several secondary rooms and the sanctuary. At the back, a niche shows the Pharaoh sitting between *Amun* and *Ra-Harakhty*. The entire structure is however very deteriorated because it was transformed into a chapel during the Christian era. With regards to **Maharraqa**'s single hypostyle room, it served as a temple of the Roman era dedicated to the Alexandrian god *Sarapis* and the goddess *Isis*. As for the last monument, consecrated to *Thoth*, god of **Pnubs**, it comes from **Dakka**, the ancient Greek town of **Pselkhis,** 25 miles north of its present location. Its construction which dates to the turning of the third century B.C. is the work of many sovereigns, in particular the **Meroe** king *Arkamani*, the pharaohs *Ptolemy IV* and *Ptolemy VIII*, as well as the Roman Emperors *Augustus* and *Tiberius*. At the time of disassembly, many of the stone blocks were found to have been dated, which shows that the temple was built with material taken from an edifice built by *Hatshepsut* and *Thutmose III*.

At **Gerf Hussein**, 56 miles upriver from **Aswan** on the west bank of the Nile, stood the "Temple of *Ramesses*, beloved of *Amun*, in the Domain of *Ptah*". Built by *Setau*, then viceroy of **Kush**, it consisted of both a built part and a part excavated into the mountain, and was referred to by the term **hemispeos**. An alley of sphinxes gave onto a courtyard which was bordered by pillars and decorated with giant statues of *Ramesses II* in the guise of *Osiris*, great god of the dead. As one entered into the **"holy of holies"** at the back of the temple there opened a niche which sheltered statues of *Ptah*, of the deified *Ramesses II*, of *Ptah-Tatenen* and of *Hathor*. Due to lack of time, the temple could only be partially saved: the structure disappeared beneath the waters, and

only the bas-reliefs and the sculptures were removed and placed in museums.

Next come the temples of **Dendur** and **Tafa**, given to the United States and Holland respectively. Since 1978, the first temple sits in a specially built wing at the **Metropolitan Museum of Art** in New York and the second stands in an interior courtyard at the **Museum of Leyde**. The most interesting one, **Dendur** is dedicated to two "saints", *Peteese* and *Pihor*, deified individuals from the 26th Dynasty. This type of cult dates back to the Ptolemaic era for the benefit of people drowned in the Nile. One can only speculate as to what drove the patron, in this case the Emperor *Augustus*, to build this sanctuary in such a remote location. The most likely reason for the building to be found here is that the two brothers, Petiesis and Pihor, drowned in this very place. The temple is small, consisting of three small rooms in a row and decorated with scenes of offerings addressed to both local gods and the gods of Nubia and Egypt: *Osiris*, *Isis* and *Horus*, but also *Arensnuphi*, god associated with *Shu* and *Onuris*, and finally *Mandulis*, the god particularly worshipped in this region of Nubia.

The Pavilion of Qertassi

Before being moved, this pavilion was 22 miles south of its present location. It was taken to the new site of Kalabsha, beside the Aswan dam. Unfortunately, only a small part of the original building remains: two pillars whose capitals, called hathoric, are decorated with the head of the goddess Hathor, and four columns topped by composite capitals. Its age is uncertain as only some inscriptions in Demotic, Greek and Coptic remain. Nevertheless, the building's many similarities to the Pavilion of Trajan in Philae allow dating it back to the Roman era.
The Pavilion of Qertassi,
Roman era,
New site of Kalabsha,
Upper Egypt.

Some 10 miles south of **Aswan**, one could formerly visit the temple of **Debod**, dedicated to the Theban *Amun*. However, since 1968 one must travel to a garden near the Royal Palace in Madrid in order to see it. It appears to be a temple of the Meroitic era built by the king *Adikhalamani* in the III c B.C. and enlarged by the *Ptolemaic* pharaohs and decorated under *Augustus* and *Tiberius*.

The journey along the banks of **Lake Nasser** ends with **Kalabsha**, situated a few hundred feet from the **Aswan** dam. The temple of **Kalabsha** itself, ancient **Talmis** to the Greeks, is a building constructed under *Augustus* for the Nubian god *Mandulis*. A walkway, extended by a flight of stairs, leads to the entrance pylon of the temple where one finds a courtyard, a hypostyle room and a **naos** composed of three decorated interior rooms. Certain texts have become famous, notably, the decree of king *Silko*, inscribed in poor Greek on the colonnaded wall: *"I, Silko, King of Nobades and all the Ethiopians, I returned to Talmis and Taphis twice. I have fought the Blemmyes and the gods offered me victory three against one. Now that I am king, I won't walk behind other kings: I overtake them. When those who wish to enter into war with me, I don't leave them at peace in their country unless they submit to me; because I am a lion in the low country and a bear in the high country... The princes of other countries that dare attack me, I don't leave them any respite. unless they beg me; they will never drink wine in their house because I take the women and children of all those who attack me"*. In the south corner, one finds a **mammsi**, a building designed to celebrate the birth of a god child; in the north corner there is a chapel which can probably be credited to ***Ptolemy IX***. In 1962 – 1963, at the time of its disassembly, a team of German archaeologists dated a hundred blocks coming from a doorway more than 24 feet in height, built by the last ***Ptolemys*** and completely decorated with scenes of offerings; it has been installed in a gallery of the **Berlin Museum**. Not far from there stands the small pavilion of **Qertassi**, of which nothing remains except four columns and two hathoric pillars. Finally a path leads to **Beit el-Wali**, a small temple excavated into the mountain during the reign of ***Ramesses II*** and dedicated to *Amun-Ra* and other divinities.

Following pages

Feluccas on the Nile

The felucca is the most common means of transport on the Nile. These light-hulled boats are generally long and very narrow. Usually sailed, they can also be rowed when the wind is not favourable.
The Nile,
Aswan, Upper Egypt.

THE SOUTH, UPPER EGYPT

From Aswan to Asyut

The crossing of **Lake Nasser** reaches its end. The Nile is poised to make its entry into the town of **Aswan**. But, surprisingly, it is literally blocked by a gigantic structure: the **"Sadd el'Ali"**, the "High Dam". Today it would be totally inconceivable to talk about the Nile and Egypt, the *"gift of the Nile"* according to **Herodotus**, without touching on the thorny problem of the **Aswan** dam. This creation of our century represents very little if one compares it to the fifty centuries of Egyptian history which preceded it. However the Dam has so completely changed the economic and daily life of the country and of its inhabitants that it cannot be ignored.

From immemorial time, the Egyptians have wanted to free themselves from the dependence which ties them to the Nile, and especially to its capricious floods. Indeed, Pharaonic texts often address the problem of the inconsistency of the phenomenon: the floods are totally irregular regarding their length, their volume and the time of their appearance. An overly generous flood disrupts the irrigation system and destroys houses; if the opposite occurs, the amount of land used for agriculture is reduced and the country experiences famine, known in the inscriptions as the *"years of sand banks"*.

If one believes the historical writings, the ideal height of a flood is sixteen cubits, namely, twenty eight feet approximately. In reality, the volume of the flood depends on the quantity of rain that falls on the Ethiopian mountains, afterwards feeding the Blue Nile. The powerful river pulls all kinds of volcanic debris with it, forming the fertile silt which gives the tide its importance: it inundates Egypt at the end of June or at the beginning of July, increases in August, culminates in September, and at last decreases with the first days of Autumn.

The ancient Egyptians, ignorant of the sources of the Nile, explained this phenomenon differently. They believed that the flood came from an underground cave close to the first cataract. Here three divinities reigned: *Khnum*, the ram god who spent his time fashioning humanity on his potters wheel, and *Satis* and *Anukis*, patrons of the island of **Sehel** and the cataract. Each year, these three guardians of the source of the Nile release the quantities of silt necessary to fertilize the Egyptian lands. It is *Hapy*, the personification of the flood, who brings the waters. That is why, from **Aswan** to the Delta, this god, depicted with hanging breasts and a pot-bellied stomach, is venerated in the hope of giving the country a satisfying flood.

An inscription, known by the name of **"Stele of Famine"**, testifies to this constant worry. It was carved during the Ptolemaic era, under the reign of **Ptolemy V**, on a rock on the island of **Sehel**. The character depicted is *Djoser*, first Pharaoh of the 3rd Dynasty, who complains of the long drought: *"My heart was afflicted when the Nile did not come for seven years. The grain became scarce, the grain became dry, all that we had to eat was in small quantities and every man was deprived of his income"*. After consulting the ancient documents, the sovereign knows what he must do with regards to *Khnum*. He makes an offering and to thank him, the god appears in a dream where he promises to provide Egypt with more constant floods. *"I shall raise the Nile for you. There will be no more years when the flood will be insufficient for the land."*

To make up for the irregularities of the river, the Egyptians constructed an ingenious system of dams, dikes, canals, and locks, all designed to permit the maximum exploitation of the flood.

The Nilometer of Elephantine Island

The Nilometer was invented in order to keep track of the fluctuations of the Nile waters, especially during the flood season. Situated at the extreme south of the country, the Nilometer of Elephantine Island allows the estimation of the date of the arrival, the size and volume of the flood in the whole of Egypt. Situated near the bank, south east of the island, it consists of ninety steps leading to the river and its walls are graduated in order to gauge the flood. Wall markings indicate the height of some particularly successful floods from the Roman era. In the nineteenth century, the Nilometer was improved with the introduction of a scale of Arabic measures.
Nilometer of Elephantine, Upper Egypt.

From the "Old Dam" to the "High Dam"

One must wait until the twentieth century before important projects are undertaken on the Nile. At the turn of the century, the British finance the construction of a dam, called **"the Old Dam"**, in order to control the swirling waters of the first cataract. Judged to be insufficient, the dam was heightened between 1907 and 1912 and again between 1929 and 1934, ending up as a 145 feet high structure creating a reservoir of some 17.5 billion cubic feet of water and flooding Lower Nubia for 185 miles during the flood season. In 1955 President *Nasser* decided to definitively solve the problem of the Nile with the construction of a much more ambitious dam. The project had three objectives: to control the floods and deficits of water all the way to the Delta; to produce electricity to be used for the development of Egyptian industry; to ensure the regular supply of water to the country and to increase the quantity of land under cultivation. The work necessary to bring this project to fruition was so great that the Egyptian authorities did not hesitate to call on the great world powers, the only ones capable of financing it. The categorical and irrevocable refusal of the United States led the government to nationalize the Universal Suez Canal Company and thereby acquire the funds necessary to build the dam. It was not long before this decision triggered off the Suez Crisis of 1956 with Paris, London and Jerusalem launching a quick military offensive, condemned by the United Nations. Finally, it is the Russians who took the lead and work began in 1960. On January 15, 1971, after eleven years of work, the presidents *Sadat* and *Podgornyi* inaugurate the High Dam, the **"Sadd el-'Ali"** of the Egyptians. After many discussions, a gravity dam was chosen, of gigantic dimensions: 140 feet thick at the summit, 3,430 feet thick at the base, 12,600 feet in length, 388 feet in height, and 150 million cubic feet in volume. By its sheer weight it can resist the power of the 550 billion cubic feet of water of **Lake Nasser**, over 315 miles long and between 6.5 and 20 miles wide.

After more than twenty five years, more and more questions are being asked about the benefits brought by the dam. Undoubtedly, the Nile has been tamed. The risks of drought or flooding seem to have been eliminated.

Intensive agriculture in certain cases permits of two or three harvests per year. However, negative effects continue to appear, causing complications for the Egyptian economy. The most serious of these complications regards agriculture. It must be recognized that the Nile has been deprived of its most important riches: the silt. Slowly, harvests become poorer due to the intensive use of chemical fertilizers, supposed to substitute the silt, but also due to a permanent irrigation made possible by the harnessing of the river. Moreover, before the construction of the dam, the ravaging waves of the flood had the advantage of "washing" the soil and cleaning it of its impurities; this is no longer the case and the increased salinity of the soil is making the land more sterile and therefore less and less productive. The second major worry concerns the constant evaporation of the waters of **Lake Nasser**. It was estimated that twenty one billion cubic feet of water would evaporate each year: this figure is well below the reality and should be increased to thirty five billion cubic feet. If there were a lack of rain over several years in Ethiopia, Egypt would suffer from drought just as in the past.

At the same time, there is an alarming level of erosion at work at two levels: a lateral erosion which is seen in the expanding riverbed, some 3/4 to 1 inch a year, which threatens buildings along the banks of the river and little by little eats away at the arable land; and also a marine erosion which allows the Mediterranean to advance up the Delta since the Nile no longer has the force to push back the sea. The most pessimistic estimates contend that the Delta will disappear by 2030 when it will have been swallowed up by the Mediterranean… Fish are equally at risk because the river doesn't carry anything but poor water lacking in nutrients, hence the fish disappear. What is more, predatory species, coming from the Red Sea, are beginning to appear on the banks of the Mediterranean. Concerning the problem of supplying the country with electricity, the previsions have once again been too optimistic. Egypt, which produced the equivalent of five billion kilowatt hours per year in the sixties, planned with the dam to double that production in order to launch its vast programme of industrialisation. Unfortunately, only eight billion kilowatt hours are generated by the power station every year, hindering the industrial expansion of the country. Finally, there remains the problem of parasitic illnesses which have developed violently, notably bilharzia, contracted in stagnant waters.

The Province of Aswan

Scarcely beyond the dam, the Nile reaches **Agilkia**, a small islet on which stood the temples of **Philae**. This site provokes much admiration because its rescue was something of a miracle. Certainly, the construction of the first dam, **"the Old Dam"**, had already done great harm to the *"pearl of Egypt"*. During most of the year, the temple of the goddess *Isis* was submerged, with only a few stones protruding from a flotsam of pylons and colonnades. When for barely a few weeks in the summer the reservoir was empty, one could come to admire the splendid building as a whole. Unfortunately, the technology that could have saved the temple did not exist at the beginning of the twentieth century. Sadly the temple was left to its fate…

In his great book *The death of Philae*, Pierre Loti vents his despair: *"Today, due to the dam established by the English, the water has risen. Risen, just as a tide that doesn't go out; this lake, nearly a small sea, replaces the twists and turns of the river and ends up swallowing sacred islands. The temple of Isis —who sat enthroned there for thousands of years at the top of a hill laden with temples, colonnades and statues— half emerges, alone, and soon drowns herself; it's she who appeared down there, similar to a big block, at this hour where the night begins to confuse everything […] Stop and silence; it's dark, it's cold; suddenly the noise of a heavy fall, followed by a never ending bustling: some great sculptured stone which has just fallen at this hour, to join in the black chaos below those already disappeared and the temple already swallowed up and the old Coptic churches, and first Christian towns – everything that was in times past the island of Philae, the « pearl of Egypt », one of the wonders of the world."*

With the dam of **Aswan**, it became patent that this jewel would be buried forever unless a solution was quickly found. It was the Unesco that took charge in carrying out this work; like at **Abu Simbel**, it's an extraordinary project. While some built a breakwater to protect the temples form the rising waters of the lake, others were busy remodelling the **island of Agilkia** to give it a topography identical to that of **Philae**.

Roman Remains on the Island of Philae

The area situated at the extreme north of the island of Philae is occupied by Roman remains: they consist of the gate of a town and ruins of a chapel dedicated to the Emperor Augustus. The gate, which leads to the Nile by a small landing, is quite well preserved. As for the chapel, there remains only some eroded and fragmented blocks to hint at its previous existence.
Roman Arch,
Roman era,
Philae, Upper Egypt.

The Island of Elephantine

On the Nile, there is no trip greater than the one which allows you to return to Elephantine, a small island opposite the town of Aswan. The trip, which takes place in a felucca, offers a sublime vision of the river and the whole of the region, surrounded by its quarries of rose-coloured granite. Today, Elephantine does not play the role it did in the Pharaonic era. At that time, the island possessed a temple dedicated to Khnum, guardian of the sources of the Nile. An inscription, under the name of "Stele of Famine", describes the importance of this island: "There is a town in the middle of the water; the Nile surrounds it: it's called Elephantine... It's the seat of Ra when he decides to give life to each one; a gentle way of life is the name of his place and the two gulfs is the name of the water. This is the twin lifeblood which gives everything... Khnum sits there like god, his sandals placed on the waves." Although very damaged, the temple is still visible, allowing one to understand what the Nile and the flood represented in the ancient era.
Island of Elephantine, Upper Egypt.

As this difficult work comes to an end, the blocks from the different temples are very carefully disassembled and numbered, then methodically transported and reassembled on the new site. Eventually, it will take eight years to return to *Isis* of **Philae** a temple like the one given to it by the Ptolemaic pharaohs.

Some blocks found in the foundations of *Taharqo* permit the dating of the site to the 25th Dynasty, but the most ancient monuments established on the island of **Philae** only date back to the 30th Dynasty. In fact, the real expansion of the worship of *Isis* to **Philae** is due to the Greek pharaohs. They destroyed and renovated old constructions, then built a temple that matched the height of their dedication to *Isis*. Little by little, they chased all the inhabitants from the island in order to consecrate it completely to Isis, the most popular of Egyptian goddesses of the Ptolemaic era. **Philae** saw its greatest hour of glory in the first century A.D. when Egypt was yielded to the Roman Emperors. Despite the decree issued by *Theodosius* at the end of the fourth century which condemned paganism throughout the Empire, the cult of *Isis* subsisted for a long time on the island of **Philae**; here the last followers of the Egyptian religion came to seek refuge. The temple of *Isis*, which had escaped Roman control thanks to its location in the extreme south of the country, ended up being condemned by *Justinian* in 551 A.D. Pharaonic Egypt just passed away for ever.

Leaving behind the *Isis* of **Philae**, the Nile then reaches **Aswan**, the city where the features of the land result in the creation of the great dam. In the last century, **Aswan** sheltered the holidays of Egyptian citizens coming from all over the country to relax and unwind. The building of the dam attracted thousands of people like a magnet. They would work either on the dam's building site, or on any Unesco-led project to rescue the temples. Afterwards, all this labour force was restructured: some were oriented towards the industries directly issuing from the creation of the dam, others towards tourism. At **Aswan**, the sudden rapid development of the latter activity is due to the moving of the Nubian temples: at last, **Abu Simbel** and **Philae** become easily accessible. As for the buildings reassembled along the banks of **Lake Nasser**, only some cruise ships, of which the most prestigious is the *Eugenie*, allow access there. Despite its expansion, **Aswan** remains one of the nicest towns in this Valley, thanks to its tranquillity and natural setting. Here the river flows along the wide corniche

sheltered by tall green palm trees. It is here, at sunset, where the Egyptians and tourists come to relax. Further on, you will reach the immense bazaars, which by their colours and multitude of smells evoke the art of life in the East.

At the time of the Pharaohs, **Aswan** was but a working town, put under the supervision of the governor of **Elephantine**; today, this relationship is reversed. At a time when the economic life of the whole of Egypt depended on the Nile and its floods, it seems altogether natural that **Elephantine** played an important role. As a matter of fact, outside the residence of the governor of the province, the island sheltered a temple dedicated to *Khnum*, the guardian of the sources of the Nile, where people from all of Egypt came to pray to the god to grant the country a satisfactory flood. Not far from the places

of worship, a ninety-step nilometer, the most important one ever built, forecasts the volume of the next flood, allowing the authorities to fix the exact tax rate and the quantities of water granted to each province. Now, surrounded by palm trees, flowered trees and antique ruins —last remnants of the height of **Elephantine**—there stands a small village of fishermen and felucca sailors that enjoy the passing of quiet days on the banks of the river.

In times past, while aristocrats, civil servants and business men basked on the island, **Aswan** was faced by the ancient town of **Souanou**, which swarmed with thousands of workmen employed in the granite quarries. It was there that, for more than three thousand years, the Pharaohs had the stones drawn that were necessary for the construction of their monuments. It is difficult to

imagine how the single province of **Aswan** was able to provide such a quantity of material, especially when one realises that there is not a temple in Egypt without its share of construction blocks, of obelisks, of pillars, of **naos**, of columns, of statues and colossuses of granite. An obelisk, 147 feet long, abandoned during the course of extraction because of a crack, shows the technique used by the ancient quarrymen to extract these enormous blocks from the mountain. Notches were cut around a previously marked surface, into which pieces of wood were inserted; the pieces were then soaked with water, splitting the rock in the desired place. The extracted block, perfectly smooth, was sent to the engraving and polishing workshops where the first trimming of the rock took place. The transport to the north was done by raft or felucca during the flood periods when the Nile was at its highest.

Finally, from **Aswan** one leaves for the land of the south. Point of departure for expeditions to Africa or Nubia, the town received the notables who travelled under orders of the Pharaoh to the cataracts in search of precious materials or rare and exotic products; as an evidence of this there is an extraordinary letter found in the tomb of a man called *Horkuf*, governor of **Elephantine** in the 6th Dynasty. It tells how he was sent by *Pepy II*, then a child, to the land of **Iam** —the name given then to Nubia— on a quest for a pygmy:

"You have said that you have brought back a pygmy from the country of the inhabitants of the East horizon for the god dances, that is like the dwarf which the treasurer of the god Urjededba brought back from the land of Punt in the time of Izezi. You have said to My Majesty that never has its like been brought back by anyone but those who have travelled Iam before. Come by boat to the Residence at once. Leave the others and bring with you the dwarf... My Majesty hopes to see this dwarf more than the products of Punt. If you arrive at the Residence, while this dwarf is with you, alive, safe and sound, My Majesty will bestow on you a greater reward than that given to the treasurer of the god Urdjededba in the time of Izezi."

It is unknown when exactly the island of **Elephantine** faded in the face of the growing power of **Aswan**. In all likelihood, the island must have lost its influence when the cult of *Khnum* began to diminish and fade. This reversal, no doubt quite late, does not date beyond the Ptolemaic era or perhaps the Roman era. In these times, it is said that swarming crowds pressed into **Aswan** on the day of the summer solstice to admire the vertical shafts of sunlight: they came to conclude that the Tropic of Cancer passed some 44 miles south of the town. This explains the reason why the scholars of the classical era used **Aswan** as a base for their calculations of the surface of the earth.

Kom Ombo, Edfu and Esna

Past the region of **Aswan**, the Nile turns with determination towards the heart of Upper Egypt. It is a strange country it passes through. The river plunges into the desert at one moment only to take to the valley at the next; as if regretting, it shakes off the arid and desolate land for the most lush and verdant oases. On the route which leads to **Thebes**, the valley of the Nile has two distinct characteristics. Sometimes it attains a width of over 12.5 miles and spreads out with pride over fields of sugar cane, vegetables and fruit trees, especially date palms. Other times, the river is almost non-existent; it becomes trapped between the Arabian desert to the east and the Libyan desert to the west, which prevent any vegetation from taking hold. Quite often, these changes take place without the smallest transition: over hardly a few dozen feet, one leaves a valley of brilliant colours to find oneself in the heart of a desolate, ochre-hued land. Here, only the few cool oases which occasionally dot the Nile are inhabited; the arid and inhospitable zones are abandoned to the wild animals and to the vultures.

25 miles separate **Aswan** from the first palm grove, **Kom Ombo**, unarguably the largest and most beautiful until **Thebes**. This did not elude the ancient Egyptians, who precisely chose this site to build the temple in honour of the gods *Sobek* and *Haroeris*. Situated on the east bank of the river, the temple enjoys an exceptional location: it gives directly onto the Nile, thus dominating the entire palm grove. The first peculiarity of this building lies in its dual character.

This particular layout, unique in all Pharaonic history, responds to a purely theological necessity as the temple is dedicated to two very different triad divinities. The left half of the temple, to the north, is reserved for the falcon god *Haroeris* —"*Horus* the Great" or "*Horus* the Ancient"— the goddess *Tasenetnofret* —"the Good Sister"— and the son god *Panebtawy*, "the Master of the Two Lands". The right half of the temple, to the south, is reserved for the crocodile god *Sobek*, the goddess *Hathor*, and for the son god *Khons*. In point of fact, but for the **"holy of holies"** located at the back of the temple and composed of two separate rooms, the building is not entirely divided in two. At the heart of the structure the two hypostyle rooms and the three vestibules form the common parts into which one enters via two gates situated on either side of the main axis. Thus, when one stands in either *Sobek*'s or *Haroeris*'s temple, and looks out towards the Nile, one sees perfectly clear the row of doorways leading into the building and to the **"holy of holies"**. The building of the sanctuary dates back to the Ptolemaic era, particularly to the reigns of *Ptolemy VI* and *Ptolemy XII*.

Kom Ombo

At the heart of the great palm grove of Kom Ombo, located about 25 miles north of Aswan, lies a sanctuary dedicated to the crocodile Sobek and the falcon Haroeris. The former protects man against the hostile powers which haunt the swamps; the latter is a warrior god entrusted to destroy the enemies of the Sun. The originality of this temple lies in its peculiar layout: it is consecrated to two different divinities, and was split into two parts. Only the entrance and the first courtyard, built right on the banks of the Nile, are shared by both cults; immediately after, the building is divided: the south half is reserved for Sobek, the north one for Haroeris.
Temple of Sobek and Haroeris, Ptolemaic era, Kom Ombo, Upper Egypt.

Greek Egypt was the result of the conquest of the country by *Alexander the Great* in 333 B.C. Contrary to all expectations, he is welcomed as a liberator because he frees Egypt from the Persian yoke. He was even better received when, shortly after his arrival, he travels to **Siwa**, a small oasis in the Libyan desert, to consult the oracle of *Amun*: who recognises him as Master of the Universe and Son of God. In the eyes of everyone, this journey seems a sign of the reverence in which he holds the national pantheon. *Alexander* adopts the Pharaonic title and entrusts to one of his lieutenants, *Ptolemy*, son of *Lagos*, the government of Egypt. Upon his death ten years later, *Philip Arrhidaeus* is crowned Pharaoh while *Ptolemy* retains the control of the government. Eventually, *Ptolemy* takes the royal title in 305 B. C. and founds the Ptolemaic dynasty, also known as the Greek or Lagid dynasty. For three centuries, until the battle of **Actium** in 31 B.C. when Egypt becomes a province of the Roman Empire, the country accepts its new Pharaohs, the *Ptolemies*. They adopt almost all the Egyptian customs, worship the gods of the Nile Valley —*Sobek, Haroeris, Horus, Hathor, Isis, Hapy...*— and have temples erected to them after the purest Egyptian style. In these temples, reliefs depict traditional scenes where the Pharaoh, wearing the high composite crown and the royal loincloth, offers water and bread to the gods; these in exchange bestow the sign of **ankh**, the symbol of life. The numerous Ptolemaic temples that exist in Lower Egypt —**Kom Ombo**, **Edfu**, **Philae**, **Dendera**...— were thus built to replace previous temples generally dating back to the New Kingdom. Being the most recent of all Pharaonic temples, they are on the whole all very well preserved.

When leaving the palm groves of **Kom Ombo** the valley narrows to such a point where soon it becomes non-existent. The **Gebel el-Silsila**, or "Chain Mountain", makes its entrance on the scene: here the abrupt and steep cliffs plunge directly into the Nile, preventing the oasis from developing. Not far from a **speos,** carved by *Horemheb* in the 18th Dynasty, lie many rocks from the Ramesses period; they tell us that this site was consecrated to the god *Hapy*. This may seem strange and paradoxical, as this divinity symbolises fertility and fecundity, two concepts quite foreign to **Gebel el-Silsila**, where everything has an air of abandon and desolation. At the time of the Pharaohs, this region was often returned to as it was the site of important sandstone quarries.

Horus to Edfu

Out of all the temples in the valley of the Nile, Edfu is the best preserved and the most compact. It's so complete that it gives the illusion of having been abandoned only recently. However, the building dates back to Ptolemy III in 237 B.C. It was finished one hundred and eighty years later: the inscription on one of the walls shows the date December 5, 57 B.C. Contrary to the many Egyptian temples remodelled over the centuries and reigns, this one was originally so well built, that the plan is perfectly harmonious: no other building needed be added here or there, nor were any later additions made that would break its original unity.
Horus Temple,
Ptolemaic era,
Edfu, Upper Egypt.

51

From the New Kingdom, this sandstone was used to build temples. It therefore seems highly probable that in **Tura** or in **Aswan** all life revolved around the quarries, by which worker's villages and small popular temples stood.

Suddenly, the Nile widens again. The last foothills of the Libyan mountains leave the river, allowing crops to take the place of the desert. On the other hand, the Arabic mountains stay with the Nile, offering the onlooker a countryside of rare beauty. When trekking along this route in Upper Egypt, it's certainly exceptional to be able to contemplate these mountains so close. The subtle blend of colours varying from yellow ochre to gold is breathtaking, especially at sunset; its neat forms, overhanging the narrow oasis, stand out against the reddening sky, which slowly fades to leave a faint glimmer of moonlight.

Soon, at the heart of this stunning landscape, the pylon of a temple is outlined in the distance: here the territory of **Edfu**, kingdom of the falcon god *Horus*, begins. The images of the *Description of Egypt* show that, at the time of *Bonaparte*'s campaign in 1798, the building was almost buried, so much so that only the tops of the entry pylons, the terrace and the upper part of the colonnades stood out. It has been cleared, but a part of the present village stands higher than the temple by several feet. This surprising sight is quite normal in Egypt; one seldom fails to notice that the level of the dwellings is greater in height simply because newer buildings are built on top of their predecessors.

If one were to visit only one temple in Egypt, without out a doubt it would be **Edfu**. Due to its excellent state of preservation, **Edfu** gives the impression of having been hastily abandoned a few days or at most a few years before. The entry pylons, the courtyards, the rooms, the passages, the vestibules and the **"holy of holies"**, all these elements have reached our time nearly intact, bereft of the smallest flaw. The texts reveal the precise date of its foundation, August 23, 237 B.C., under *Ptolemy III Euergetes I*, and that of its inauguration, too: December 5, 57 B.C., under *Ptolemy XII Neos Dionysos*. Despite its late era, the temple of *Horus* retains, along general lines, the characteristics of buildings from the Pharaonic era. Elsewhere, certain novelties

appear, no doubt inherited from the Greek origins of their patrons. Contrary to the constructions of the New Kingdom, the Ptolemaic temples are distinguished by their exemplary clarity of design: the monumental entry pylon, the portico-lined courtyard, a series of hypostyle rooms leading into small cult chapels, and a **naos**, inside which, hidden from view, stands the statue of the god. The entire structure is protected by a surrounding double wall, the first made of stone and the second, much more massive, of raw brick. All this was constructed so that the **naos**, commonly called **"holy of holies"**, became the most central room, the most intimate, the highest from the ground with the lowest ceiling, and therefore the darkest. Parallel to this new organisation of space, the architecture is weighed down with superfluous architectural elements that make the buildings look enormous: developed grooves, imposing architraves, composite capitals, colonnaded walls… The reliefs and the texts acquire a rigorous organisation: the registers, clear and straight, are marked by inscriptions neatly arranged in columns. Finally, the shapes acquire previously non-existent curves and the costumes are enriched by sundry ornaments drawn from Egyptian iconography; the symbolic meaning of this images tends, however, to become blurred over the course of the reigns, leaving only an ornamental rationale behind them.

At **Edfu**, one honours *Horus Behedety,* a particular avatar of *Horus,* especially worshipped as a royal sun god. *Horus* is considered as the protector of the Egyptian kingdom; in his turn, the Pharaoh becomes the representative of *Horus* on Earth. In the Ancient era, the temple of **Edfu** would become once a year the scenario for a particular ceremony: *Hathor* was leaving her temple at **Dendera**, situated 38 miles down the river, to go and greet her husband *Horus Behedety*. To do this, the goddess had to come by way of the Nile, a journey which lasted four days. The reunions took place in a chapel situated north of the city; there *Horus* waited for his partner at the eighth hour of the new moon's day on the eleventh month of the year. The merrymaking lasted for fourteen days of the crescent moon: thus was celebrated the mythical marriage of the couple which was accompanied by rites, visits to temples, sacrifices and solemnities. Finally, at the end of a great banquet attended by all the inhabitants of the region, *Hathor* returned to **Dendera** until the following year.

Some miles further, at the spot where the Nile makes a slight turn eastwards, the impressive ruins of **el-Kab** stand at the foot of the Arabic range. **El-Kab**, the **Nekheb** of the ancient Egyptians, is the town of the vulture goddess *Nekhbet*: she protects Upper Egypt like the cobra goddess *Wadjit* symbolises Lower-Egypt. The first traces of the habitation of this site date back to prehistoric times, but it's especially from the New Kingdom that the cult of *Nekhbet* developed. From the beginning of the 18th Dynasty, the city of **Nekheb** became the capital of the 3rd nome of Upper Egypt, and the Pharaohs embarked upon enormous architectural projects. The city, essentially composed of a religious area and a living area, is surrounded by a great wall, amazing in size. It forms a square made of raw brick and measuring 1,925 feet per side, 42 feet thick and 21 feet high. The temples occupy the south-west quarter of the great walls, which are very damaged. Yet several distinct structures can be descried, notably the great temples of *Nekhbet* in the east and *Thoth* in the west. *Thoth* appears here as the spouse of the vulture goddess. As for the town, nothing remains: it was sacked and pillaged during the last century by seekers of **sebakh**. This is an untranslatable Arabic word: in fact it describes a specific place, having ancient ruins whose earth is used as fertilizer for cultivated land. Beyond it lies a small village, **Esna**, which hides a temple whose ruins are sunk in a gully thirty feet deep, so much has the level risen over the centuries. Of the Roman sanctuary built by ***Claudius*** and ***Vespasian***, only the hypostyle room, very well preserved, has withstood the tests of time.

The Theban Region

From the province of **Aswan**, the Nile has travelled around ninety five miles through an Egypt sometimes lush and overpopulated, sometimes desert-like and, in fact, deserted. For the great majority, the inhabitants of Upper Egypt are **fellahs**, an Arabic word describing peasants, people of strong bodies, thick hands and weathered skin. For numerous generations they have tried to take the best from the land of the Nile. From **Aswan** to **Luxor**, apart from their daily farming chores, the fellahs also try desperately to conquer the pitiless desert. The results are positive since very often, the palm groves that dot the valley on either side of the river are the result of

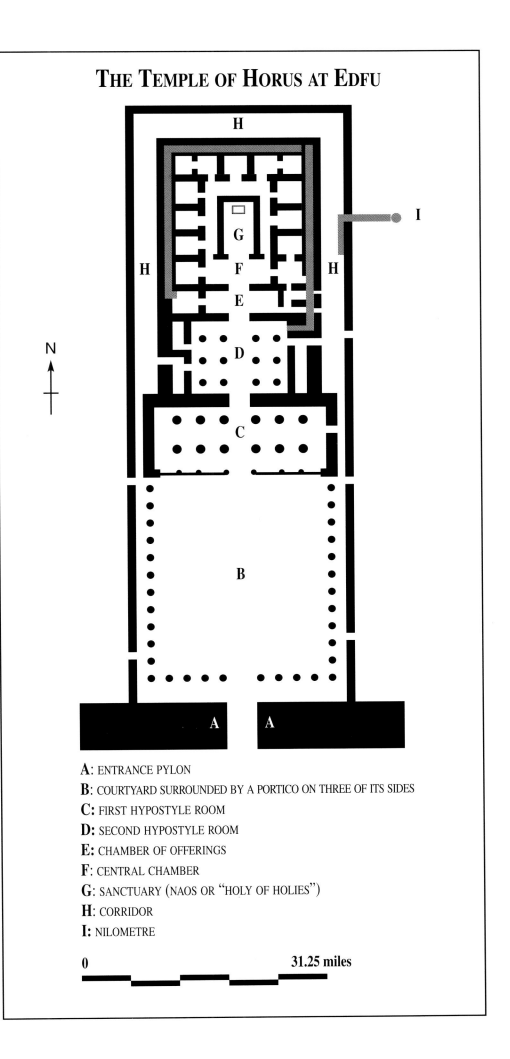

THE TEMPLE OF HORUS AT EDFU

N

A: ENTRANCE PYLON
B: COURTYARD SURROUNDED BY A PORTICO ON THREE OF ITS SIDES
C: FIRST HYPOSTYLE ROOM
D: SECOND HYPOSTYLE ROOM
E: CHAMBER OF OFFERINGS
F: CENTRAL CHAMBER
G: SANCTUARY (NAOS OR "HOLY OF HOLIES")
H: CORRIDOR
I: NILOMETRE

0   31.25 miles

this incomparable effort at intensive irrigation. At **Kom Ombo**, for example, it seems that more than 28,000 acres have been reclaimed from the desert in this fashion. Sugar cane in particular is grown and has become one of the main crops of southern Egypt since the beginning of the nineteenth century. In this region, not only is sugar harvested, but also refined in the gigantic sugar refineries of **Erment** or **Kom Ombo** which have transformed this changeless land into an industrial site. From the unused stocks of sugar cane, a white coloured juice is obtained that is highly appreciated there as its taste quite resembles that of sugar water.

From **Esna**, the valley of the Nile becomes bigger and not once more surrenders to the Libyan and Arabic ranges. Sometimes to the west, sometimes to the east, sometimes on both banks of the river, fields spread as far as the eye can see: vegetables, wheat, cotton, sugar cane, orchards of date palms, fruit trees typical of African regions —mangos, guavas, palm trees, pomegranates, lemon. The best way to travel in the **Luxor** region is to take the Nile. Apart from the many old fashioned cruises organised by travel agencies, there is a better means of transportation, slower, but much more picturesque: the felucca. Feluccas are spacious boats, equipped with high sails, which move lazily at the whims of the winds and the currents. The trip is fascinating, because it allows one to discover, at any time of day, the different faces of the river and the valley: the desert hills visible on the horizon or the palm groves stretching along the river, spreading diverse colours which blend wonderfully with each other.

Where the Nile just turns lightly to the east, a city appears in the distance that was the very symbol of the Egypt of the pharaohs: **Luxor**, the *"City of the Hundred doors"* that *Homer* sang in antiquity. The expansion of this modern town is quite recent; less than a century ago, only a few establishments welcomed the adventurous and wealthy travellers who for three or four months, set out on the conquest of the ancient East. Indeed, this growth really dates back no more than thirty years, corresponding with the development of "mass tourism."

It is a tourist boom for **Luxor,** which is full of luxury hotels, restaurants, bazaars and souvenir shops. From the four corners of the planet, one hastens to

The Temple of Amun at Karnak

The largest religious site in the Nile Valley, the temple at Karnak is consecrated to Amun, the god of the Empire, to the goddess Mut, his spouse, and to the son god Khons. Its disordered and chaotic appearance is due to the fact that from the 12th Dynasty to the Greco-Roman era, generations of sovereigns have built there, adding in a rather haphazard manner a courtyard, an obelisk, a boat landing, a pylon, a chapel... The heart of the temple dates back to the 18th Dynasty. Unfortunately, this is the most dilapidated part of the site. The entrance pylons have collapsed; only two obelisks remain, the most distant one was the work of Thutmose I, the other that of the Queen Hatshepsut. The latter measures a hundred feet in height and is considered one of the most beautiful in the Nile Valley. It was erected by the Queen in honour of her jubilee.
The Temple of Amun at Karnak, New Kingdom,
East Thebes, Upper Egypt.

contemplate the remains of a civilization re-emerged from the abyss thanks to the work of *Bonaparte*, *Champollion* and their successors. Unfortunately, the city has completely changed, losing in the process much of its charm due to the constant flood of tourists. Certainly, most of the city's revenue comes from tourism, but the pressure put on the visitors menaces this nascent industry, necessary for the health of the economy. However, despite the existence of enormous hotel complexes which are spreading further and further south every day, certain parts of the city have managed to retain their charm of former times. In particular, the centre of the city, dating from the nineteenth century, where beneath a shaded corniche stroll passing visitors, romantic couples, boatmen, trinket sellers and felucca or carriage drivers. On the other hand, in the heart of the modern city, the action never stops. In a continuous hubbub, modest stalls offer, for a nominal fee, souvenirs, essences, perfumes and spices whose heady scents blend and combine with others more enticing like grilling herbs and meats. In the middle of all this excitement there are carriages, cars, buses, pedestrians, farm animals, carts, donkeys and cows, all moving in perfect disorder towards unknown destinations.

The Oarsmen

This relief, which comes from the temple of Amun at Karnak, shows oarsmen in a boat that archaeologists succeeded in reconstructing. These vessels are powered by oars, one row for each side, and a sail in the form of a trapezoid. In order to steer two different systems are used: two large oars trailing on each side of the stern or a single tail oar. The hull, generally made of wood, is held together with ropes or wooden pegs and made watertight with resin. The deck is equipped with cabins whose size and number depend on the size of the craft. The modernisation of the Egyptian fleet does not date beyond the Lower Era due to the influence of the Greeks and the Phoenicians.

Temple of Amun at Karnak, New Kingdom, East Thebes, Upper Egypt.

However, in the midst of this swarming confusion, the ruins of the temple of **Luxor** stand impassive and immutable. Luxor was built in the Pharaonic era to celebrate the **Opet Festival**, which marked at the beginning of the season of **Akhet** —or flood— the Egyptian new year. On such occasion, the Theban god *Amun* left his domain of **Karnak** to travel to the temple of **Luxor**, situated two miles upriver. The festivities lasted several days, twenty seven according to sources from the Ramesses period. After several ritual celebrations in **Karnak**, the god of the Empire, *Amun,* his spouse, *Mut,* and their son god, *Khons,* were placed on a golden boat carried by a procession of priests and followed by a jubilant crowd with tambourines and sistrums, and set off towards the Nile, among chants and sacred hymns. The procession followed the river to **Luxor** where the triad of gods came to take their place on a temporary altar created for this occasion. At the end of these solemnities, divinities, priests and the faithful came together in the temple of **Karnak**. On the whole, this building dates from the New Kingdom. The layout of the building is very

simple. From the beginning, *Amenhotep III*, founder of the temple, foresaw a temple surrounded by annexes, the **"holy of holies"** and a hypostyle room entered by a monumental doorway which faces north. A large courtyard with a portico preceded by a pylon was added. No doubt later, a double row of seven columns enclosed by a second pylon was also added to the temple which henceforth was entered from the East. Later on, *Ramesses II* intervenes and builds another courtyard in front of the column, slightly turned towards the east due to the course

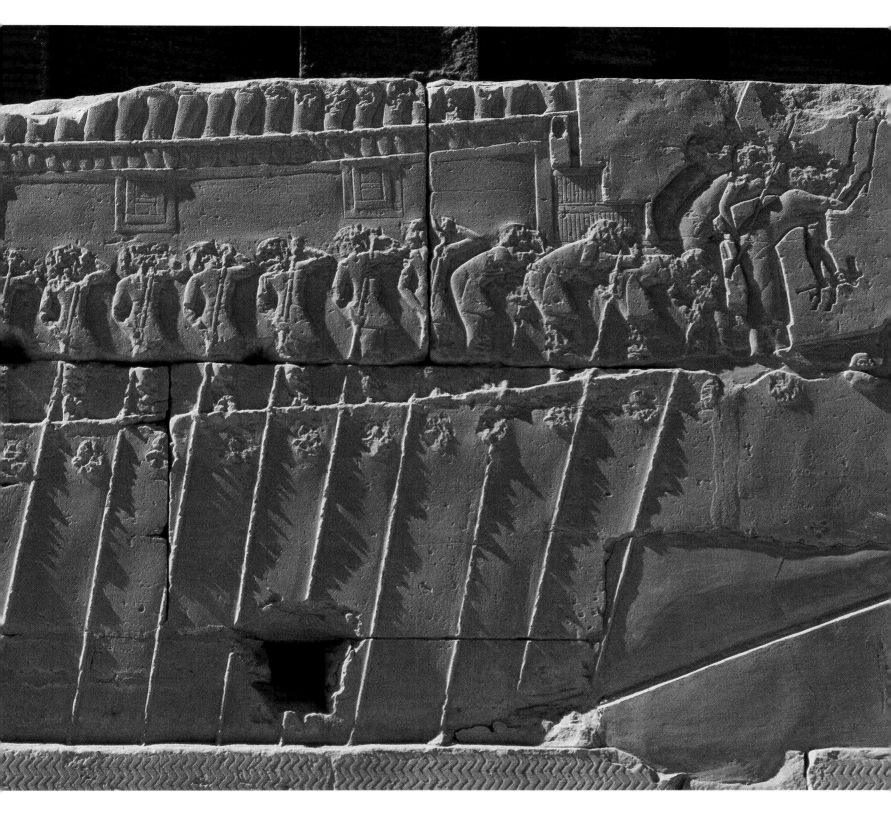

of the Nile. This is preceded by a monumental pylon at the foot of which he installs six colossal statues bearing his effigy and a pair of obelisks.

The history of these two monoliths is a reverberating one. To pay homage to *Champollion*, who came to elucidate the mystery of the hieroglyphics, the government of *Mehemet Ali* decides to give France one of the two obelisks of **Alexandria**, better known as "*Cleopatra*'s Needle." However, during his trip in Egypt in 1828-

1829, *Champollion* returns to **Thebes**. There he discovers the obelisks of **Luxor**. Instantly, he makes a decision. On July 4, 1829, he sends his brother a letter which unmistakeably concludes: "*It's one of these obelisks of Luxor which needs be transported to Paris; there is nothing better than to have both of them*". The negotiation lasts several months; finally, on May 18, 1830, *Mehemet Ali* gives France the two obelisks of **Luxor**. Due to the difficulty involved in moving the blocks, only the western obelisk was transported to Paris. This choice was guided by the advice of **Champollion** who in September 1829 sent the following report to the Minister of the Navy: "*If, unfortunately, one is reduced to importing only one of the obelisks of Luxor, it is necessary, without a doubt, to take the western obelisk, the one on the right upon entering the palace. The pyramidion has suffered slightly, it is true, but the entire body of the obelisk is intact and in an admirable state of preservation*". Finally, on October 25, 1836, the obelisk is erected in Paris's "Place de la Concorde" under the care of the engineer **Lebas**. In 1980, the French government definitively renounces its rights to the second obelisk; in 1998, the obelisk of the "Place de la Concorde" sees its summit endowed with gold leaf.

The route of the corniche then leads to the immense field of ruins at **Karnak**. It consists of the main temple of *Amun, Mut*, and *Khons*, the Theban triad. The origin of *Amun* is quite mysterious. Some say that he is one of the eight primordial gods of the cosmogony of **Hermopolis**; some think that he is a divinity native of Middle-Egypt; while others accord him purely Theban origins. Whichever the case, it is necessary to wait for the beginning of the Middle Kingdom for *Amun* to begin to impose himself. Rapidly, he becomes the national and dynastic god, the uncontested master of the Egyptian pantheon. Thus the clergy elaborate a new theology directly related to his new prerogatives. In this text, we learn of a serpent named *Kematef,* which at the beginning of time emerges from the primordial chaos to begin the process of creation. Once his task is accomplished, he creates *Irta* and then sleeps forever. Following the work of her progenitor, *Irta* conceives the earth in the same way as eight gods who over the course of a long journey, will give birth to the Sun. Their mission complete, the eight gods return to **Thebes** where, like *Kematef* and *Irta,* they plunge into an eternal slumber. At **Thebes**, *Amun* appears under the signs of *Kematef;* in this way, he becomes the creator of the Theban cosmogony. Until the end of the Ptolemaic era, *Amun* enjoys a highly developed cult, although from the beginning of the Lower Era, his prestige tends to fade away. There is no doubt that the height of his power took place between the 18th and 19th Dynasties during which the temple of **Karnak** did not cease to be enlarged and embellished.

Of all the temples of the Nile Valley, the one of **Karnak** remains the most difficult to visit due to its complexity. Today, it is a disorganised jumble of successive constructions of which most are additions, replacements or superimpositions which forbid a logical visit to the site. The domain of *Amun,* surrounded by a thick wall of raw brick, consists of two main axes, each one displaying a series of monumental pylons: six, numbered I to VI and arranged from west to east, and four, numbered VII to X, from north to south. This is a random, imaginary numbering, as it follows the order of a visit to the temple without taking into account the real chronological sequence; it's only used for the sake of convenience. In fact, each pylon of the east-west axis corresponds to a phase of enlargement of the site and marks the entrance of the temple in a given era. Before the temple of the 12th Dynasty, over the course of many reigns, courtyards, pylons, secondary temples, stores, chapels, altars for sacred boats, and obelisks were added. Thus, the temple is entered by its most recent parts: throughout the visit, one goes back in chronological order to more primitive buildings as one goes east. Outside these two buildings, the walls of *Amun* contain an enormous sacred lake with a promenade and a temple dedicated to *Khons,* the son god of the Theban triad. The marvel of **Karnak** resides in the hypostyle room of the New Kingdom, situated between the second and third pylons. The sight is both dazzling and imposing. It consists of a hundred and thirty four columns distributed in a room which measures 370 feet long and 185 feet wide. The lighting comes from **claustra** windows. The system consists of building a room of which the ceilings are at a different height. This allows the fitting, between the lower and upper ceilings, of a series of hemstitched windows which filter the light. At **Karnak**, the twelve central columns measure nearly 80 feet in height, while the one hundred and twenty two remaining columns are a third shorter: the difference in height is used for this ingenious system of windows. The room was begun under the reign of **Amenhotep III**, who, in all likelihood, constructed the twelve central columns. At the end of the 18th Dynasty, **Horemheb**, adds the lateral columns and the second pylon which, from then on, closes the hypostyle room. As for the décor, it dates mostly from the reigns of **Sethos I** and **Ramesses II**, even though, from time to time, other royal names appear like **Ramesses I**, **Ramesses IV** or **Ramesses V**. To the north of the domain of *Amun,* opens the enclosure of *Montu,* the warrior god of the Empire; unfortunately, it is very damaged.

**Hapy,
the Genie of the Nile**

This androgynous character, with hanging breast and a bloated stomach, is called Hapy, a personification of the Nile flood. He symbolises abundance and fertility, assures fertile lands, and guarantees Egypt a satisfactory harvest. He is generally depicted kneeling, yet keeping within arm's reach the products of the Nile, or vases containing water. The ankh crosses hanging from his arms symbolise life.
The open air Museum
of Karnak,
Altar of Hatshepsut,
New Kingdom,
East Thebes, Upper Egypt.

From the tenth pylon, the last of the north south axis, an alley of sphinxes 1,000 feet long leads to the enclosure of *Mut* which consists of a temple, unfortunately badly damaged, and a crescent-shaped sacred lake. Here, *Mut* is identified with the goddess *Sekhmet*, the lioness, yet she incarnates the pacific aspects of this destructive and dangerous lioness. The two goddesses eventually merge as their personalities are opposed but they also complement each other. To relieve the destruction of *Sekhmet, Mut* intervenes as the warrior goddess. It is in honour of this ambivalent divinity, both *Mut* and *Sekhmet,* that **Amenhotep III** ordered the construction of the temple at **Karnak**. According to the texts, he was stricken by an incurable illness and in asking to be cured, he made an offering of six hundred effigies of the lioness *Sekhmet* to the temple of *Mut*. The most deteriorated of them are still visible on the site, while the most beautiful have been transported to Egyptian or European museums.

The domain of the god of the Empire is not limited to the temples of **Karnak** and **Luxor**. *Amun* enjoys the immense riches administered by his clergy and totally outside the control of the central government. All victorious campaigns add to his wealth because, as a form of thanks, the Pharaoh presents the god with the bulk of the war booty and the annual tributes of the vanquished territories. From the New Kingdom, *Amun* becomes the first economic power in Egypt. If one believes the texts from the Ramesses period, more than eighty one thousand people worked in his service during the 19th Dynasty. It is understood that not all the people entrusted with the running of the temple belong to the clergy. Some are in charge of the purely economic organisation of the temple: the management of the god's properties and riches, the collecting of taxes, the relations with other temple... Others are farmers, scribes, artisans, policemen, musicians, singers, gardeners... At the top of the hierarchy stood the high clergy. It consisted of the chief priest of *Amun,* certainly the most powerful man in Egypt besides the pharaoh, the "god's fathers", the "pure priests", the **kheryhebet**, a man who holds the program of the ceremonies on a scroll, and the members of the **unuyt**, an eminent college of priests. At the same time, the lower clergy welcomes the secondary priests, the "purifiers", who sometimes give the daily service at the

temple but who, more often, deal with earthly chores. The temple opens its doors at daybreak thus allowing the entrance of those priests responsible for the morning ceremonies. Once purified, the officiant enters into the **"holy of holies"** and breaks the seal of the **naos** all the while reciting chants and hymns of adoration. After having burned incense around the divine statue, he proceeds to the ceremony of the opening of the mouth by which the god recovers, every morning, the powers of sight and speech. *Amun* then receives a meal composed of meat, assorted vegetables, bread, cakes, beer and wine. The god absorbs the invisible material of the food and becomes imbued with the spirit of these presents; then, his meal is placed on the altars of the secondary divinities before being consumed by the priests. Thus restored, the god can perform his ablutions. The priest extracts the statue from the **naos** in order to wash it, to purify it, to dress it, to perfume… The god can now return to its receptacle until the lunch service which merely consists of some sprinkling of water and the burning of incense. At sunset, the morning services are repeated and the statue is returned to the **naos**, sealed for the night.

When one leaves the temple of **Karnak**, on the west bank of the Nile, the golden contours of the Libyan range show in outline in the distance, the hills chosen by the kings of the New Kingdom to carve their tombs and build their funerary temples built, called "Castles of Millions of Years". The Nile, more than half a mile wide at this point, gently flows between the two temples with majestic indolence. It divides those living from those that lived, as if denying any possible confusion between the world of the living and that of the dead. To reach the west bank of the river one must take a boat as, oddly enough, not one bridge spans the Nile between the towns of **Edfu** and **Qena**, about 95 miles apart. **Luxor** is far from both, although, from sunrise to sunset, ferries, boats, feluccas and barges ply from one bank to the other, taking all kinds of people, animals and vehicles in a hustle that defies belief. On these floating bridges, women wrapped in their black cloaks, **fellahs** with shuffling footsteps, idle children, overloaded cars and trucks, all mingle with the tourists, truly astounded yet at the same time amused by the unusual spectacle. On the other side of the Nile, the same confusion welcomes the crowd.

Luxor

Located on the eastern bank of the river, Luxor is nowadays the town that welcomes visitors to ancient Thebes. Right by the shore stands the sanctuary of the Theban triad: Amun, Mut and Khons. The layout of the temple shows in a most distinct manner: the obelisk (preceding the entrance to the building), Ramesses II's large courtyard (recognisable by the mosque of saint Abu el-Haggag, built on the east side during the Arab era), the double, seven-pillared tier, and finally the buildings of Amenhotep III (large courtyard and temple).
Temple of Luxor,
New Kingdom,
East Thebes, Upper Egypt.

Barely has the boat reached the bank when each one, with no exception, is sucked into a hustle of chaotic jostling and shoving, strident hooting of horns, shouting and bellowing. All of a sudden, once the landing is over, an arresting calm ensues as one enters the Libyan desert. A few scattered houses, occasionally grouped in little villages, stand along the route leading to the foot of the cliff. Whitewashed to shelter its occupants from the sun, they proudly bear on their façades crudely made drawings which at first can be surprising: one sees representations of boats, horses and sometimes planes, at whose sides always the same building is depicted which resembles a mosque with high minarets. These are the dwellings of the **"hadj"**, a name given to those Muslims who have performed the pilgrimage to **Mecca**, and who commemorate their voyage on what they value the most: their houses. The idea seems pleasing, and apparently has caught on, as even the factories making carpets, papyrus and alabaster objects, boast on their rough white walls similar designs reproducing scenes taken from the tombs of kings.

Beyond, lies the Theban necropolis. During the Pharaonic civilization, the west was reserved for the land of the dead and the east for the land of the living. This is why the towns and the cult temples are found on the east side of the Nile, while the necropoleis stand on the west bank. Evidently, this rule would not have been applied in all cases; there are some exceptions especially from later eras. Here, the rule is observed. The temples of **Karnak** and **Luxor** dedicated to the cult of *Amun* stand in **East Thebes**; it is also there that the Egyptian population lived at the time of the Pharaohs. In **West Thebes** lies the city of the dead with its royal and civilian tombs, as well as its funerary temples.

Suddenly, on the right side of the road, two isolated statues stand like two gigantic sentinels: they are the **"Colossi of Memnon"**, last vestiges of the funerary temple of *Amenhotep III*. The statues measure some 68 feet; each one has been carved from a single block of sandstone taken from the town of **Heliopolis**, located some 435 miles upriver. They were named later and there is no direct connection with *Amenhotep III*. Historians tell that in the year 27 B.C. the north colossus cracked following an earth tremor. The stone started to vibrate and make a hissing sound due to the abrupt changes in temperature which would ensue after daybreak. For a long time, a rational explanation was sought for this

strange whistling. It must have been in vain, since a legend was established. This long moaning sound was attributed to the wailing of *Memnon*, hero of the Trojan war killed by *Achilles*, when he greeted his mother *Eos*, Aurora, at sunrise. From all parts, people came to hear the colossus, arriving at daybreak in order not to risk missing a single instant when the hero's moaning could be heard. At the beginning of the third century, *Septimus Severus* decides to restore the damaged statue which henceforth becomes mute although it still retains the name.

On the west slope of the mountain, two desert valleys, accessible by a narrow rocky passage, shelter the royal hypogea: the **Valley of the Monkeys** to the west and the **Valley of the Kings** to the east. Nearly all the pharaohs of the New Kingdom, from *Thutmose I* to *Ramesses XI*, were buried in this place protected by Hathor, the "Dame of the West". In total, sixty two tombs have been accounted for. They are of unequal importance: the least interesting consist of simple anepigraphic excavations while the most prestigious ones bear witness to the power of their owners. Some measure more than three hundred feet long. Generally, they consist of a door carved into the rock, a gently sloping passage flanked by small niches, some secondary rooms, or one or more funerary chambers of varying dimensions. The walls, decorated with scenes taken from the royal funerary books, recount the fate of the royal soul and its voyage in the underworld: the **"Book of Opening of the Mouth"**, the **"Litany of Ra"**, the **"Book of that which is in the Netherworld"**, the **"Book of Gates"**, and the **"Book of Caverns."** The results lack neither originality nor charm. What a wonder it is to see all the images which, from one end of the cave to another, set the scenes of a thousand strange creatures armed with pikes and swords, genies, gods and goddesses proceeding with the pharaoh through the nocturnal provinces.

However, despite the provisions taken by the royal authorities, almost all the tombs of the **Valley of the Kings** have been pillaged. The site bursts with such riches that, since the 20th Dynasty, it has attracted bands of thieves. The waves of arrests and trials which accompanied the first crimes didn't succeed in solving the problem, so much that *Pinudjem*, the third "king-priest" of the 21th Dynasty, decided to save the royal mummies by hiding them, either in the tomb of *Amenhotep II* or in a small cave carved into the cliff of *Deir el-Bahri*.

The Theban Region

Today, the ancient name is intentionally used to describe the region that homes the site of this sumptuous Pharaonic capital: Thebes, the City of the Hundred Doors. On the eastern side of the river, seen from afar, one finds the temples of Luxor and Karnak: the bank of the living amongst ancient Egyptians. These days such still seems to be the case, as modern towns in this region are located on this bank of the Nile. On the western side, however, near the Libyan cliff, life is less denser: for the ancient Egyptians, that was the bank of the dead, known under the name of Theban Necropolis. It includes all that the society of the New Kingdom could fancy in order to serve its dead ones: tombs carved into the cliff, both royal and civilian, and funerary temples. Appearing here from behind are the "Colossi of Memnon": they mark the site of the funerary temple of Amenhotep III.
Colossi of Memnon,
New Kingdom,
West Thebes, Upper Egypt.

Numerous prestigious Pharaohs, notably *Amenhotep I*, *Tuthmosis III* or *Ramesses II*, rested there until 1881, the year in which the hiding place was discovered thanks to the research of the French archaeologist *Maspero*. Only one tomb, discovered in 1922 by *Howard Carter* and his patron, *Lord Carnarvon*, had escaped the pillagers of Antiquity: it was the tomb of *Tutankhamun* whose fabulous treasure has endlessly excited the fantasy of travellers.

From the **Valley of the Kings**, a path leads to the temple of **Deir el-Bahri** built by *Senenmut* for the Queen *Hatshepsut*. This type of temple plays a specific role: daily rituals take place there which are intended to assure the afterlife of the deceased. In Ancient Egypt, death is not the end but a step towards a new form of existence. However, this passage is highly perilous, because when death occurs, the elements constituting the human personality disperse, each conserving its integrity. These elements, some spiritual, some material, include **akh**, invisible power, **sekhem**, spiritual energy, **sakh**, the spiritual body, **ba**, the soul, **ka**, the manifestation of conservative and creative energies, **khet**, the material body, **ib**, the heart and **ren**, the name. Thus, the second life is not possible, unless all these elements meet, the most fragile being the body which must be successfully preserved via mummification. This existence in the underworld occurs like all terrestrial life: the deceased sleeps, participates in festivities, works, drinks, eats… Whatever these activities may be, a second death must be avoided at all costs for this would be definitive. He cannot elude food and drink, without which no one can survive, so they are regularly brought to him in the funerary temple, built for this purpose.

No sanctuary blends in with its environment more harmonically than Queen *Hatshepsut*'s at **Deir el-Bahri**. The unity between the building and the rock circus is so perfect that the cliff seems to have been tailored to receive this majestic construction. Three terraces bordered with porticos and connected by ramps, create this uncommon building; they lead to several chapels dedicated to funeral cults of the queen and of her parents, *Thutmose I* and *Ahmes*, as well as of *Amun*, the god of the Empire, and *Ra-Harakhty*, the Sun god. From one part to the other of the next terrace, there are two small areas for cult purposes: the first is consecrated to *Hathor*, the protector of the Theban necropolis, the second to *Anubis*,

god of mummification. The walls of the temple are covered with scenes, superbly engraved in bas relief and painted, evoking the essential events of the reign of *Hatshepsut*: her divine birth when she proclaims herself the daughter of *Amun* and queen *Ahmes*, her expedition to the land of **Punt**, from where gold, essences, exotic products and perfumes were imported, and the ceremony of the erection of the obelisks in the temple of **Karnak**.

Going southwards, one notices the small village of **Deir el-Medina**, the only inhabited place in the entire Theban necropolis. Here lived the workmen charged with the carving, the fitting, and the decoration of the royal hypogea. They lived in the most complete isolation to avoid the spreading of information about the contents or location of the tombs. Placed under the direct authority of the highest official of the necropolis, the vizir of **West Thebes**, they were closely watched by militia and nubian police. The archaeological excavations revealed two lots of **ostraca**: one among the rooms' rubble, the second one inside a well. These fragments of limestone portray in a very precise way the daily life of this particular community: the running of the village, the labours, the trials, the crime, the corruption, the strikes, the inheritances. One learns, for example, that a certain *Amenonah*, suspected of pillaging the tomb of *Ramesses III*, had been acquitted through lack of evidence. Much later, at the time of clearing of the sepulchre, the archaeologists removed, partially by chance but with much surprise, the object of the theft adroitly hidden in the cave. Thus one can read hundreds of testimonials and anecdotes about the life of this community. Next to the village stands the necropolis made up of tombs created by the workmen during their spare time. Although they are not all of equal size, a common layout can be identified: the superstructure is composed of a courtyard leading to a funerary chapel placed on a small pyramid made of brick and capped with a stone pyramidion; the interior structure of the temple consists of a shaft, filled in on the day of the funeral, which gives access to a cave where the possessions and the sarcophagus of the deceased are placed. Some of these tombs are very well preserved, boasting painted decoration often inspired by the iconographic patterns of the great royal hypogea. As a general rule, the cave is ornamented with scenes taken from the "**Book of the Dead**", while the chapel contains scenes of an openly religious significance.

Deir el-Bahri
The funerary temple of Queen Hatshepsut, the "Castle of a Million Years," is built at the foot of the Libyan escarpment, beneath a rocky circus with which it blends in. Indeed, no other building in Egypt integrates so perfectly into its surroundings. Built by the Senenmut, chief architect of the queen, the temple consists of three terraces joined by ramps. It is dedicated to the divine guardians of the beyond, the Theban triad and to the deified Hatshepsut.
Temple of Queen Hatshepsut,
Dier el-Bahri,
New Kingdom,
West Thebes, Upper Egypt.

The Expedition of Punt

The walls of the funerary temple of Queen Hatshepsut at Deir el-Bahri are decorated with scenes outstanding by their originality and finesse. On the south wall of the intermediate terrace one finds the account of a naval expedition led by the Queen in the ninth year of her reign in order to bring, from Africa, products unavailable in Egypt, such as rare animals, precious stones, scented trees, panther skins, myrrh... It describes the trip to the land of Punt (Somalia or Yemen?). Certain reliefs of this composition show Egyptian soldiers, their arms full of frankincense trees, crossing the river in which several species of fish swim.
Deir el-Bahri,
New Kingdom
West Thebes, Upper Egypt.

The path to the west enters a small valley where the remains of the princes and royal spouses rest: it is the **Valley of the Queens**, also known as the "Place of Beauty." Eighty tombs are to be found: some are heavily deteriorated, others are simple anepigraphic excavations; the latter feature among the great master-pieces of Theban painting. The most beautiful of all these tombs has recently been opened to visitors: it is the sepulchre of the Queen *Nefertari*, Great Royal Spouse of *Ramesses II*. Her tomb has benefited from a long process of restoration compelled by to major problems: humidity and earth tremors. Today, it has recovered the freshness of yore and boasts images of an exceptional elegance: *Nefertari*, bearing the vulture's wing of the goddess *Mut* and a long linen robe, venerates the divinities of the Egyptian pantheon and makes them offerings. Here she is seated beneath a canopy and plays **senet**, the ancient form of backgammon; there she is standing, her hands joined in adoration before *Maat, Osiris*, the guardians of the beyond or other personalities of the divine world; yet elsewhere there is a human-headed bird which symbolizes her soul. Apart from this superb cavern, two other tombs deserve to be noted; belonging to two sons of *Ramesses III* which died at a very young age, they are *Amenherkhepeshef*'s and *Khaemwaset*'s sepulchres. The reliefs, embellished with brilliantly coloured paintings, stand out by their naivety as they were intended for children. The two brothers are introduced by their father to the gods of the underworld: *Osiris, Isis, Ptah, Thoth*, genies with the head of a jackal, an ibis…

Spreading across the plains or carved into the sides of the Libyan range, the civil necropoleis of **Dra Abu el-Naga, Asasif, el-Khokha, Sheikh Abd el-Qurna** and **Qurnet Murai** are home to several hundred tombs built by nobles of the New Kingdom; these include some of the highest officials of the country —viziers, high priests of *Amun,* the viceroys of Nubia—, those close to the king because of their duty —inspectors, heralds, cupbearers—, and important officials, such as royal scribes, inspector generals, etc. Sometimes, notables of less influence feature among the owners of the tombs: architects, surveyors, minor administrators, scribes and secondary inspectors, astronomers. Except for certain architectural variants and diverse qualities of execution, a common plan shared by all the tombs can be determined. A decorated courtyard leads to a cave carved out of the cliff face. It is composed of a primary chamber, long but not very deep, and decorated with scenes relating to the earthly life of the deceased. The walls are flanked by a religious stele to the south and a biographical stele to the north. A door cut into the thickness of the western wall leads to a second chamber, long and narrow, at the end of which there is a niche cut into the wall that shelters a statue of the deceased. Here the decoration is more overtly funerary: the creation of the mummy, the "opening of the mouth" ceremony, the funeral procession with the transport of the catafalque of the deceased on the west bank of the Nile, the banquet… This leaves the cave, very often anepigraphic and made accessible by a shaft carved in the second chamber. It is here that the

66

mummified corpse and any possible funeral treasures rest. A work written on papyrus or on leather accompanies the deceased to the great beyond; it consists of the **"Book for coming forth by day"**, more commonly known as the **"Book of the Dead"**. It compiles the formulas and incantations, with accompanying illustrations, designed to assure the resurrection of the deceased by warranting his usefulness in the underworld and therefore his securing total freedom of movement. All the known copies of this book are not identical; some contain chapters that are missing in others. In total, there are one hundred and ninety different chapters, some of them eloquently titled: "How to live after death", "How to enter the underworld and how to leave it", "To avoid the decomposition of the body in the underworld", "How not to die a second time", "To ward off demons", "To avoid the capture of the soul in the beyond", "To come back and visit your house", "To avoid the defunct's heart robbery"…

Finally, three funerary temples, the famous "Castles of a Million Years", stand majestically and grandiosely at the edge of the desert. From north to south, one finds the small temple of **Qurna**, built by *Sethos I* at the beginning of the 19th Dynasty. Unfortunately very damaged from being used as a quarry for a neighbouring village, it still possesses very elegant, finely carved reliefs, characteristic of the royal art at the dawn of the Ramesses era. Further on lie the ruins of **Ramesseum**, the **"tomb of Osymandias"**, according to *Diodorus*

Siculus, if one follows his judgement, the temple should be the most impressive of all the Theban necropolis; today it consists of a chaotic scattering of ruins. Built to serve the funeral cult of the most prestigious Pharaoh of the New Kingdom, *Ramesses II*, its layout was a classic one: courtyards and hypostyle rooms follow one another all the way to the **"holy of holies"**, surrounded by annexed rooms. In the first courtyard stood a colossal statue of the king, 62 feet in height, 24.5 feet wide, with a weight of more than 1,016 tons. It is said it was already roughly treated in ancient times; nowadays, only debris partially covers the courtyard. Still further south, rises the temple of **Medinet Habu**, modelled for *Ramesses III* after the temple of **Ramesseum**. Only the monumental entrance is different. It has a basement, unique in a building of its kind in Egypt; it conforms to the dictates of the **migdol**, the name given to fortified gates by Syrians, with crenellated towers fitted with windows. Besides its unusual gateway, the temple is interesting in many ways. In fact, it is the best preserved building of its type in the whole Theban necropolis, offering the best insight into the procedure of a royal funeral cult. Elsewhere the reliefs engraved on the walls, of particularly excellent execution, constitute a documentary source of prime importance regarding the end of the Egyptian New Kingdom. The texts, highly detailed and proffusely illustrated, recount the battles of *Ramesses III* against the Aegean-originated "People of the Sea", and against the Libyans, as well as different military campaigns in Nubia and the Near East.

West Thebes unveils to us its most intimate secrets. On this bank of the Nile, entirely devoted to the industry of death, the most glorious Pharaohs of Egyptian history have left their mark. The study of the necropolis of Thebes has served to make these sovereigns more familiar and accessible, but along with them, hundreds of other characters have also come to light: *Rekhmira*, vizier of *Thutmose III*, *Senenmut*, chief architect of *Hatshepsut*, *Kheruef*, steward of *Tiy*, or *Sennedjem*, *Inerkhau* and *Ipuy*, the three artisans of the necropolis under the **Ramesses**…

Abydos

Leaving **Thebes** the Nile takes its route through a valley that spreads out on both sides of its banks. Strangely, it appears a little helpless: it makes curves, long and sinuous, as if an irresistible force attracted it towards the east. Never does the river approach the Red Sea so much as at this point. As the crow flies, it is hardly a hundred miles which separates **Qift**, the ancient **Koptos**, from the port of **Qoseyr**. The ancient Egyptians had already learnt to exploit this opening on the **Sinai** and to Asia in order to develop trade with the people of the Red Sea: from **Koptos** expeditions left for the rock quarries of the Arabian desert, particularly **Wadi Hammamat** where shale was exploited. Slightly to the north, the Nile abruptly changes direction. From **Qena** to **Nag Hammadi**, the powerful Arabic range obliges the river to make a long meander, a good 30 miles to the west, before heading serenely towards the north. Facing the town of **Qena**, a name which refers equally to the province of which it is the chief town, one finds the temple of **Dendera**, domain of the goddess *Hathor*. She is one of the most complex figures of the Egyptian pantheon, inasmuch as she adopts diverse forms and functions. Represented by a cow or a woman with a two-horned head piece holding the solar disk, she is the daughter of *Ra*, considered as the eye of the star, and the spouse of *Horus*. She intervenes as the protector of the Theban necropolis, minder of the royal children, mistress of foreign countries, lady of **Punt** and of **Byblos**, mistress of the turquoise, goddess of love, joy and dance, goddess of sycamore, mistress of ballets and of cheerful refrains, lady of ebriety… Her attributes are impressive and her powers unlimited. At **Dendera**, *Hathor* possesses a temple of the Ptolemaic era. Like the one at **Edfu**, it is very well preserved and

shows a great unity of composition, but here the figures represented on the walls are superior both in quality and in content. Unusual scenes, mostly astronomical, decorate the ceilings of the different rooms: immense paintings depicting the vault of the heavens, the hours of the day and night, the celestial regions, the decans, the decades, the planets, the cardinal points, or the constellations. The rooms give onto the decorated "crypts", of which there are twelve at **Dendera**. This term does not have the same significance as in Western vocabulary; it denotes the small chambers fitted into the thick walls or foundations which were used for the storage of sacred and divine objects, the riches of the temple and the implements for the cult. Two **mammisi**, one constructed by *Nectanebo*, the other by *Augustus*, stand at the main entrance to the temple. This word, of Coptic origin, signifies "place of birth" and refers to the small buildings in which the birth of infant gods, and, by extension, of the infant king, namely, the Pharaoh, were customarily celebrated. The enclosure of **Dendera** includes a sacred lake; it symbolises the primordial waters, the *Nun,* out of which emerged the Sun god, hence life itself, at the dawn of creation. This temple is the best preserved of its kind. Four stone stairways descend into a vast basin where the water has disappeared and given way to palm trees. During ritual ceremonies, the priests would carry there the sacred boats of the gods and would purify them. Outside the sanctuary, small children offer wheat seeds to visitors which two thousand years later are thus recalled of the essential purpose of **Dendera**: to worship the cow *Hathor,* goddess of fecundity and abundance.

Between **Dendera** and **Nag Hammadi**, the Nile follows its course to the heart of sugar cane and cotton fields, abundantly irrigated by a system of dikes and canals. Finally, after **Nag Hammadi**, home of one of the most important sugar refineries in the country, the river comes to itself. Except for a few hesitations, it heads for the Mediterranean Sea by the north-west route. From the village of **Balyana**, a road 6 miles long leads to the ancient city of **Abydos**.

Located on the border between the fertile valley and the Libyan desert, **Abydos** is the largest holy city of the Pharaonic period and was consecrated to *Osiris*, the god of dead. The legend explains how *Osiris*, son of *Geb,* the Earth, and *Nut*, the Sky, inherits the terrestrial kingdom from his father. He teaches men agriculture; he gives

The Temple of Medinet Habu
South of the Theban necropolis, between the ruins of Malgata and the route coming from the Nile, lies the site of Medinet Habu. It consists of different cult places, the best preserved and the most important being the funerary temple of Ramesses III. Strongly influenced by the neighbouring temple of Ramesses II, the Ramesseum, this construction stands out by its colossal aspect which initially can appear a little overwhelming. However, after having entered the enclosure of the temple, one quickly notices that the enormous size of both the building and its décor does not preclude a genuine balance in proportions.
Temple of Ramesses III,
Medinet Habu,
New Kingdom,
West Thebes, Upper Egypt.

assassinate him. Thus he invites *Osiris* to a great banquet
gathering seventy two guests, his accomplices. During the
meal, he brings a trunk which he promises to give as a gift
to anyone who can fit into it exactly. When *Osiris* lies
down inside, the accomplices rush to the trunk, seal it and
throw it into the Nile. *Isis,* sister and wife of *Osiris,* sets
out to look for him. She finds him in the port of **Byblos**
and decides to bring him back to Egypt hiding him in the
marshes of the Delta where she avails herself of the
opportunity to conceive a son by her defunct husband, the
future *Horus.* But *Seth,* made aware of these events by his
accomplices, returns to the Delta where he discovers the
body of *Osiris:* he cuts him into pieces and disperses
them throughout the country. For the second time, *Isis*
travels the Valley of the Nile looking for his precious
remains. To help her in her search she calls in her sister
Nephthys and the jackal *Anubis.* Once they gather the different pieces, they put the corpse back together and wrap
it in bandages, thus creating the first mummy. Then, *Thoth*
and *Isis* return him to life, but from now on *Osiris* reigns
in the kingdom of the dead. At the site where each part
was found, a temple was built; it is said **Abydos** would
have kept the relic of his divine head.

During the entire Pharaonic period, **Abydos**
benefited from an unparalleled prestige. Under the two
first dynasties, the kings and high officials had themselves buried in this place, in the sepulchres of raw brick
preceded by a limestone stele, indicating their names.
From the end of the Old Kingdom, the cult of *Osiris*
developed and **Abydos** became the first holy town of
Egypt. Rapidly, pilgrims stream from all parts to seek the
grace of the god. Before leaving their places, they leave a
stele, of greater or lesser quality depending on their
social level; it commemorates their voyage in order to
help them accede to eternal life. Hundreds of monuments
of this kind were found in the nineteenth century and
taken to museums all over the world. Unfortunately, very
little remains today of this great spiritual place. Only
three buildings, quite damaged today, have stood the test
of time. The most beautiful and the best preserved one is
the temple of *Sethos I*; its is a peculiar status for it is neither a cult temple nor a funerary temple. It could possi-
bly be a splendid offering from the sovereign to *Osiris*.
The temple is dedicated to seven divinities, each of them
requiring a specific cult place. The layout of the building

was therefore conceived to fulfil these demands: from
the exterior courtyards to the most intimate rooms, the
architect respected this division into seven parts; from
the entrance to the end of the temple, seven corridors
lead to seven chapels where, at the end of the ceremonies, the sacred boats of the deified *Sethos I*, of *Ptah*, of
Ra-Harakhty, of *Amun*, of *Isis*, of *Osiris*, and of *Horus*
were kept. In reality, nothing is more seductive to the eye
than these reliefs finely carved in a limestone of un-
blemished purity. All the characters have a respectful air
in their gestures; here the art of the relief reaches perfec-
tion. Some rooms, which have preserved their poly-
chromy, a rare thing in Egyptian temples, allow us to
imagine the magnificence of these cult buildings at the
time of their construction. The second hypostyle room
leads to a passage whose walls bear one of the two
famous **"King list of Abydos"**. This is a list of all the
kings, seventy in this case, who, from *Narmer*, first Pharaoh of the 1st Dynasty, to *Sethos I*, second Pharaoh of
the 19th Dynasty, ruled Upper and Lower Egypt. It is
very interesting to note that several sovereigns have
disappeared: for example, in the 18th Dynasty neither the
queen *Hatshepsut,* nor the Pharaohs of the Amarnian era
(*Amenhotep IV – Akhenaten*, the young *Tutankhamun,
Smenkhkara* and the God's Father *Ay*) are featured.

The **Osireion** extends slightly south of the temple
of *Sethos I*; it is unfortunately very deteriorated. This
building, a subtle mix of white limestone, pink granite
and golden sandstone, is no other than the tomb of *Osiris* and its layout resembles that of all Egyptian tombs.
However, a thick vegetation prevents access to the passages decorated with the royal funeral books; only the
funerary chamber remains visible at the top of the
mound. Lastly, around a thousand feet away, stands the
temple of *Ramesses II*. Of lesser dimensions than his
father's, and nowadays even more deteriorated, the
temple has the same purpose: to commemorate his pilgrimage to the holy city of *Osiris*, as any other mere
mortal erecting his simple stele.

Leaving **Abydos,** its ruins, its legends and
its gods, one enters the province of **Sohag** famous for
its Coptic convents, reckoned amongst the oldest
in Egypt: the **Deir el-Abyad** (the "White Convent")
and the **Deir el-Ahmar** (the "Red Convent"). Both date
back to the fourth century and share a similar layout,

The Pilgrimage
at the Mecca

*Egyptian village houses are
often decorated with colourful
images and a naïve style that
reveals a deeply rooted Muslim
tradition. They represent the pilgrimage to Mecca performed by
the owner of the building, either
man or woman. Upon returning,
these people, who are called
"hadj" or "hadja", paint the
most memorable scenes of their
trip on the outer walls of their
houses. The most frequent
representation shows the pil-
grim in front of the Kaaba, a
cubic stone at the centre of the
mosque of Mecca around which
Muslims walk and pray. In the
Koran, it is said that the "Black
Stone" embedded in the wall
was brought to Abraham by the
archangel Gabriel.*
House of "Hadji",
Upper Egypt.

with a ceremonial hall which opens onto a vast basilica closed to the west by a small vaulted chapel and a baptismal font. **Sohag** possesses a very numerous Coptic community whose blending with the Muslim population is often rather deficient. This has occasionally triggered riots and rebellions, always very difficult to suppress because of their violence. Opposite, on the east bank of the Nile, stands the town of **Akhmim**, consecrated in ancient times to *Min*, god of fertility. Recently it has become a centre for craft activities. In its schools, the teachers instruct young children in the techniques of weaving and pottery. For them the Egyptian divinities pose no secrets as they tirelessly reproduce scenes inspired by Pharaonic history.

THE CENTRE, MIDDLE EGYPT

From Asyut to Fayum region

The geographical division of Egypt into two different regions, the South and the North, dates back to the most distant antiquity. At the dawn of Pharaonic history, *Narmer*, from **Hierakonpolis**, a town between **Esna** and **Edfu**, succeeds in vanquishing the people of the North; once the task of the unification of Egypt is complete, he proclaims himself "King of Upper and Lower Egypt", thus affirming his power over the two kingdoms of which the country is comprised. This victory is commemorated on an object kept at the **Museum of Cairo**, a votive schist palette known as the **"Narmer palette"**. On its back, *Narmer*, whose name features at the top of the palette, is depicted seizing a prisoner by the hair and about to strike him with a club; as a headpiece, he wears the white crown of Upper Egypt, or **hedjet**. On the front, the same king can be seen by a khol-grinding jar, this time bearing the red crown of Lower Egypt, or **deshret**. Followed by a sandal-bearer and preceded by a scribe and four standard-carriers, all of shorter height than himself, he marches towards two rows of five prisoners each. Later, the Pharaohs adopted a single crown which combined the white crown of Upper Egypt and the red crown of Lower Egypt; this was the **pschent** —the **sekhemty** of hieroglyphics—, which translates as "the Two Powers". This duality between North and South shows everywhere, especially in the royal titles, namely, the series of names chosen by the pharaoh on the day of his investiture and aimed to describe and distinguish him from his predecessors and his successors. His second name, the **"nebti"** name or the **"He of the two ladies" name,"** guarantees him the tutelage of the two protective goddess of Egypt: *Nekhbet,* the vulture goddess of Upper Egypt, and *Wadjit,* the cobra goddess of Lower Egypt. In the same way, his fourth name describes him as **"He of the sedge and the bee"**, the respective symbols of North and South. Numerous instances confirm this double attachment in texts and representations. Egypt is often called the "Two Lands" or the "Double Country"; accordingly, it is under the protection of *Nekhbet,* the goddess of **el-Kab,** capital of the South, and *Wadjit,* goddess of **Buto,** capital of the North. The lotus of the South provides a contrast with the papyrus of the North, just as the bee does it with the sedge, or the white crown with the red crown. Yet the designations of "upper" and "lower" do not necessarily correspond to a geographical reality: the town of **Aswan,** in the south of Upper Egypt, is no more than 266 feet above sea level.

And what about Middle Egypt? As a matter of fact, it is purely a creation of modern times designating the region between **Asyut** and **Fayum** region, an area of 250 miles along the Nile. Here, the valley never ceases to narrow or to widen as dictated by the Libyan and Arabian ranges, and the river is often forced to twist and curl as it meanders its way towards the Mediterranean. However, the lands of Middle Egypt have an immense advantage inasmuch as they never let themselves be completely overcome by the desert. Consequently, prairies and farmlands continuously surround the villages built along the Nile.

Soon, the river comes across an imposing dam built at the turn of the twentieth century to irrigate the lands of Middle Egypt and to supply the **Ibrahimeh Canal**; it announces the town of **Asyut**. A sluice built on the west bank allows boats to ply freely up and down the river. From here the road leads to the oases of the Libyan Desert, notably **el-Kharga**. Virtually unchanged since ancient times, it is thanks to its strategic location that the town has enjoyed a certain prosperity.

The "Castle of Pigeons"

The Egyptian countryside is dotted with rather strange constructions which at first sight can come of a surprise. In reality, they are dovecots. Often built in raw brick, then whitewashed, the façade displays several holes which correspond to small clay pots embedded in the structure and used by the birds to place their nests. In Egypt, these buildings are traditionally referred to as "castles of pigeons".
Pigeon loft, Fayum region, Middle Egypt.

The citizens of **Asyut**, the capital of the 13th nome of Upper Egypt, worshipped *Wepwawet,* a jackal-headed divinity which played an important role in funeral practices. In the **"Pyramid texts"** of the Old Kingdom, it is he who performs the ceremony of the Opening of the Mouth on the mummy of the deceased and introduces him into the underworld. On the occasion of the annual feast of **Abydos**, where the "mysteries" of *Osiris* were celebrated, a procession led the great god of the dead through the valley; he was preceded by *Wepwawet,* "He who Opens the Paths." The Greeks mistakenly took him for a wolf; unarguably, this accounts for their naming the town **Lycopolis**, or the "City of the Wolf". **Asyut** could have played a decisive role in the course of the First Intermediate Period, but the immense power of **Thebes** to the South and **Herakleopolis** to the North prevented it from fulfilling its ambitions. Centuries later, a recalcitrant Christian community, one of the most hostile to the Arab invasion, found refuge here. Thus, from then until the present day, **Asyut** has remained the region with the highest percentage of Christians among its population. Incidentally, it is also home to several nuclei of Muslim fundamentalists, against whom the Egyptian government endlessly struggles. Considered as one of the most important towns in Middle Egypt, **Asyut** possesses numerous industries, notably textiles and cement, which benefit from a constant restructuring and modernization. On leaving the town, the mountain ranges make their compelling presence be felt anew. On the Libyan side, the valley manages to assert itself, revealing crops and immense palm groves that stretch for many miles. Conversely, on the Arabian side, the cliff frequently reaches the very river, thus forbidding any development. This is why, between the towns of **Asyut** and **el-Minya,** the locals inhabit the western side of the Nile, leaving the opposite bank to vultures and predators.

Tell el-Amarna

Nevertheless, in the fourteenth century B.C., the heretic Pharaoh *Amenhotep IV* chose this somewhat peculiar site to establish his ephemeral capital: **Akhetaten**, the present-day **Tell el-Amarna**. Here, the imposing Arabian cliff slightly recedes from the bank of the river to form a vast rock enclosure some 16 miles long. No sight can prove more striking than this immense desert expanse where only the imagination is capable of re-enacting the events that took place here during the Pharaohs' time. Of the royal city, only some brick foundations remain which show the original location of temples, palaces and dwellings; these are the few vestiges of a city built in haste and suddenly abandoned twenty years later. However, despite its ruinuous state of

Fellah on the Banks of the Nile

The Valley of the Nile is characterized by the presence of rich oases spreading along the banks of the river. It is here that the peasants, called fellahs in Arabic, concentrate all their efforts, since, apart from the Delta, no other agricultural areas are to be found in Egypt. The valleys can reach 10 to 15 miles in length, although they can also become very narrow, at times almost non existent; in Middle Egypt, only the Libyan side is cultivable. Fortunately, it is very rich: sugar cane, orchards, date-palm groves, citrus fruits... Banks of the Nile, Egypt.

conservation, **Akhetaten** is the best preserved example of a "city" from the New Kingdom, as its early abandonment spared it the decay that any permanent habitation would have entailed. It is understood that the troubled historical conditions which motivated its construction do not allow **Akhetaten** to be considered as an archetypical city, but the study of the site has all the same allowed historians to deepen their knowledge of town planning during the 18th Dynasty.

Amenhotep IV is the youngest son of the queen *Tiy* and the fastuous *Amenhotep III*. During his seventeen-year reign, he left a particular imprint on Pharaonic religion and culture by raising *Aten*, visible manifestation of the solar star, to the rank of dynastic divinity.

Aten is not a creation of **Amenhotep IV**, since the name already features in the **"Pyramid texts"**. At that time, it was but one of the many facets of the Sun god Ra-Harakhty. His cult began to develop under **Thutmose IV** and **Amenhotep III**; under **Amenhotep IV**, he becomes the supreme god who lights the world with his bountiful rays, giving warmth, light and beauty, and bestowing life. Numerous theories have been advanced that seek to account for this religious upheaval: political reasons, **Amenhotep IV**'s peculiar personality, genuine religious foundations prompting the new doctrine… However, the present state of knowledge on the subject does not allow any of these theories to pre-empt the others. It is very likely that a conjunction of several factors lies at the heart of this heresy: a political context dominated by the priests of *Amun* which the royalty seeks to limit; a sincere desire to honour the Sun in its clearest manifestation, the solar disk itself; a man possessing an ambiguous personality, certainly a philosopher and mystical thinker but, above all, a fanatic. In any case, between the forth and eighth years of his reign, **Amenhotep IV** breaks definitively with the clergy of *Amun* and abandons **Thebes** for **Akhetaten,** the "Horizon of *Aten*" or the "Horizon of the Sun Disk." The name of the ancient dynastic god is abolished, as well as the plural form of the word "god", for henceforth there is but one god, *Aten*. Accordingly, he changes his name from **Amenhotep**, "*Amun* is content", to **Akhenaten**, "glory of the Sun Disk."

Egypt, Gift of the Nile

"Egypt is a gift of the Nile". *That single phrase alone summarizes Egypt's reality. Herodotus, who travelled in Egypt in the fifth century B.C., describes the country in these terms:* "The soil of Egypt does not resemble that of Arabia, which is next to it, nor that of Libya, nor even that of Syria: earth is black and crumbly because of the deposits and the silt carried by the river from Ethiopia." *In fact, the valley of the Nile has nothing in common with its neighbours' arid land. It is necessary to leave the river and its banks to appreciate the contrast between the Nile-fed valley and the rest of the country, which is but an immense desert.*
Banks of the Nile, Egypt.

Thus, **Amenhotep IV** establishes his new capital at an untouched location, *"revealed by Aten himself"*. He marks the divine spot with fourteen cave stelas that tell of his first visit to the site, his seizing power and his definitive appointment of **Akhetaten** as a city exclusively devoted to the solar disk, *Aten*. An oath accompanies these texts: *"An oath pronounced by the king of Upper and Lower Egypt, he who lives in justice, the Master of the Double Country, Neferkheperoure, Ra's Only One, the Son of Ra who lives in justice, the Master of the Diadem, Akhenaten, to whom life is given forever."* Pharaoh promises never to trespass the perimeter marked by the stelas: *"The south stela, which is in the mountains, east of Akhetaten, is the Stela of Akhetaten next to which I made a stop. I shall never go beyond it towards the south. And the southwest stela is erected exactly in front of this one, on the opposite mountain, to the west of Akhetaten."* Thus the inscription compiles a list of the different stelas and finishes with a very precise measurement

of the town: *"If one measures Akhetaten from the southern stela to the northern stela, it measures (…) a distance of 6 iteru, 1.75 khet, and 4 cubits. In the same way, from the north-west stela to the south-west stela (…), the distance is exactly 6 iteru, 1.75 khet, and 4 cubits. And the region included between these four stelas (…) constitutes the district properly called Akhetaten."*

This distance is equivalent to a little more than 7.5 miles. Within its perimeter live the king and his family as well as a part of the Court, the main ministers, high officials of the government, and numerous architects, artists, or craftsmen who, according to the estimates, numbered between twenty and fifty thousand people. The city stretches along the banks of the Nile and occupies the central part of the enclosure. An avenue, the "Royal Road", crosses the town from north to south. It is bordered by different buildings: the Royal "Great Palace", the "Great Temple", an open air temple to *Aten* called the "Temple of the *Aten* at **Akhetaten**", the principal administrative buildings and some secondary cult buildings, also dedicated to *Aten*. In this area, the "Record Office"

has left a series of clay tablets inscribed in cuneiform, most of them in Akkadian, the lingua franca of the Near East, and known as the "**Amarna** letters." These constitute the diplomatic correspondence exchanged during this era between Egypt and the independent Asiatic powers —Babylonia, Assyria, Mitanni, Arzawa to the west of Anatolia, Cyprus, the Hittite Empire— or the vassal states of Syria-Palestine. In all, they add up to more than three hundred and fifty tablets, dating from the thirtieth year of *Amenhotep III* to the third year of *Tutankhamun*, most of them from the reign of the Pharaoh *Akhenaten*. These archives are unique in their kind. Some of them attest to the difficulties encountered by the vassal states attacked by enemies of Egypt: they are desperate appeals addressed to the king, to send help to the besieged princes. Others concern the value of precious metals, diplomatic marriages or commercial relations.

Around the centre of the city, the houses of functionaries and their workshops are scattered over the north and south sections. Often the name of the owner is known: the famous sculptor *Thutmose*, who left a superb collection of finished or rough pieces, or the vizier *Nakht*. These residences were built in an anarchic fashion, lacking a structured plan. In the heart of the city, the housing followed a hierarchical rule: the god in the centre, then, proceeding outwards, the king, the high officials and the assistants. Prevailing in all dwellings is the area reserved for green spaces or gardens. The house is built around a hall of columns, single or double, sometimes preceded by a loggia; the surrounding rooms often have service rooms attached to them. Outside is the garden, its size depending on the owner's status; it separates the house proper from the workshops, the servants' quarters, the granaries and the stables. Towards the southernmost section of the town, a royal residence, the "Maru-Aten", includes, aside from the buildings reserved as dwellings, an area for cult and a vast garden with an interior lake and a gazebo. In the same way, the north end of the site is occupied by another palace, no doubt that of *Nefertiti*, spouse of the heretic king. To this day, it remains unknown why there was such a proliferation of royal residences in **Akhetaten**. It is likely that each one had a particular and well defined function, the celebration of certain ceremonies or the housing of certain members of the family demanding a specific, irreplaceable location.

Activities on the Nile

Since the Pharaonic era, the life of the Egyptians has been organised around the Nile. In the ancient tombs, numerous images show what were the pastimes and activities of the valley. Whatever the era, one notices that the illustrations are dominated by scenes of hunting or fishing in the marshes. Today, the Nile is undoubtedly less rich and has less fish than ever before, but it still plays its role as the providing father of Egypt.
Banks of the Nile, Egypt.

Far to the East, tombs of officials were carved into the Arabian cliff. They are divided into two groups: those of the south and those of the north. Despite certain variations, their layout is noticeably identical to those of the Theban tombs of the 18th Dynasty: a courtyard; two successive rooms, the first, wide but not deep, the second, long and narrow; and a niche containing the statue of the deceased. The iconography, however, is altogether different. Traditionally, hardly ever, if at all, does the sovereign feature in civil tombs. Whether it is about funeral scenes —worshipping of underworld divinities, preparation of the mummy, funerals— or images taken from daily life, the prevailing character in the representation is the holder of the tomb. Such cannot apply in **Akhetaten** where *Aten,* as the universal god, is equally in charge of the dead, usurping the prerogatives of *Osiris* and those of the other funeral gods. In this highly particular context, logic would demand that, on the walls of the tombs, the scenes show the deceased worshipping *Aten.* However, the images are dominated by the mighty presences of the king and his family worshipping the solar disk, whose rays reach hands that hold the **ankh** cross, the very symbol of the life that radiates from the Pharaoh. This is explained by this simple phrase: *"You rise in peace at the Horizon of the sky, Oh living Aten, creator of life, but no one knows you, save your son Akhenaten; you have shown him your designs and your strength."* One therefore understands that the sovereign assumes the role of official mediator: he becomes the sole prophet of his god, the representative of *Aten* on Earth and the indispensable intermediary between his god and his subjects. In this way, no one would know how to worship *Aten* directly other than the king and his family. The common folk worship *Akhenaten* who in his turn worships the solar disk since from then on it shall be the king who warrants them eternal life.

Aside from this change of iconographic themes, the tombs of **Tell el-Amarna** stand out by their particular style. In effect, the religious upheaval of the Amarnian period accompanies a radical modification of the Egyptian artistic canon. The idealism of the beginning of the 18th Dynasty gives way to an extreme realism, verging on caricature: head abnormally pulled backwards, equine face, fine-spun almond eyes, ears overly elongated, prominent nose, jutting chin, slim neck, narrow chest, thin waist, spindly limbs, feminine breasts, bloated stomach, ample hip… One easily notes that the pharaoh adopts

markedly androgynous features, although the reasons that drove him to impose these strange artistic guidelines remain obscure. The iconography has been suggested to be directly inspired by the quite unusual physical characteristics of **Akhenaten**, some even going so far as to attribute it to the symptoms of an affliction called the **"Fröhlich Syndrome"**. Nevertheless, this thesis cannot be reasonably upheld as one of effects of the alleged illness is sterility; the sovereign had several daughters, no doubt six, and at least one son, for in all probability **Tutankhamun** was **Akhenaten**'s son. The theological implications of this imagery have also been dealt with. *Aten,* as the creative divinity, is *"the father and mother of men"*; Pharaoh, the image of the god, must therefore reflect this ambivalence. This choice has been explained as the king's voluntary desire to differentiate himself from the rest of humanity. Certainly, the different divinities of the Egyptian pantheon are generally recognizable by their iconography: *Thoth* is a baboon or an ibis, *Ptah* is enclosed in a mummified form, *Min* is ithyphallic. Since **Akhenaten** represents *Aten* before his subjects, what could be more natural than proposing to his followers an unmistakeable representation of himself, namely, a realistic image of his person.

As for the tomb of *Akhenaten*, it was discovered at the beginning of the twentieth century by an Italian researcher in the cliffs overlooking **Akhetaten** to the east. Certain archaeologists believe that the king was initially buried in this tomb since, according to the findings made on the site, the funeral chamber seems to have been sealed at the moment of burial. Other researchers do not agree with this theory, due to the deplorable state of the objects found in the tomb and its surroundings: everything was reduced to rubble including the sarcophagus, the sacred vessels and the funeral statues, or **shabtis**. In point of fact, whether *Akhenaten* was buried here originally or not is unclear, but it is certain that he did not remain here for long. His body, beyond all doubt, was moved by his followers at the time of the abandonment of the city. It is unknown where to, either the **Valley of the Kings** or elsewhere. No one can really say since his mummy has not yet been discovered.

The last three years of the Amarnian era are very controversial due to the appearance of an enigmatic person: *Smenkhkara*. It is unknown what his real ties to the royal family were: was he *Akhenaten*'s younger brother? Or was he *Tutankhamun*'s older, of else half, brother? Whatever the case he seems to have been called to **Akhetaten** by the sovereign himself, then awarded the princess **Meritaten**, *Akhenaten*'s oldest daughter, as spouse and he is associated on the throne in the role of co-regent. Two years after these events, *Smenkhkara* and *Akhenaten* pass away, with but a few months intervening between each death. The rule then falls to the young *Tutankhaten*'s lot; aged nine, he carries out precisely the same deeds as his predecessor only reversely. He abandons **Akhetaten** for **Thebes**, replaces *Aten* with *Amun* and changes his name from *Tutankhaten,* "Living image of *Aten*", to *Tutankhamun,* "Living image of *Amun.*" In the **Valley of the Kings,** a sepulchre, known under the name of **"Tomb 55"**, sheds a weak light on this troubled period. Discovered in 1907 by an archaeologist working on behalf of *Theodore Davis,* it consisted of a single room mainly containing a mummy in a sarcophagus, a chapel of gilded wood, four sacred vessels, and some figurines. As the title of the work indicates, *"The Tomb of the Queen Tiy"*, *Davis* believed he had found the cave of the mother of *Akhenaten,* but more advanced studies, notably on the mummy, led Egyptologists to affirm that it was a man's body, in this case, that of *Akhenaten* himself. This thesis has been progressively abandoned, particularly due to a series of medical examinations comparatively carried out on the remains of *Tutankhamun* and of this person: everything leads us to believe that this mummy belongs to a brother or half brother of the young *Tutankhamun*, may be the very mysterious *Smenkhkara*.

Today, the modern village of **el-Hagg Qandil** welcomes the rare visitors who seek to know the ancient **Akhetaten**. However, sacked and pillaged after the death of *Akhenaten* and the return to the orthodoxy of *Amun*, the royal city does not resemble anything other than what it was before its construction: a vast arid and inhospitable area. In fact, only the common tombs, those from the south group and those from the north group, offer some interest. The royal tomb has been inaccessible for a number of years, and moreover it is very damaged. As for the town, it consists of a few eroded stones, fascinating for archaeologists but difficult for amateurs to construe. Additionally the site of **Amarna** suffers from its isolation in the heart of the Arabian desert; no tourist infrastructure can be found on its surroundings. The two nearest cities capable of offering any form of lodgings to visitors, lie 47 miles south towards **Asyut** or 31 miles north towards **el-Minya**.

Beni Hasan

As one goes towards the north, the valley becomes bigger. Here it reaches some ten miles in width, spreading out over the west bank of the river while the opposite bank remains a desert. One approaches the village of **el-Ashmunein**, called **Khmun** in the ancient era and later **Hermopolis** in the Greek era, the original name meaning "City of the Eight". It alludes to a group of eight divinities who, according to the hermopolitan beliefs, would have preceded the creation of the world: *Nun* and *Naunet*, the Primordial Ocean, *Heh* and *Hauhet*, the Infinity, *Kek* and *Kauket*, the Darkness, and *Amun* and *Amaunet,* the Hiddenness. The couples, whose female and male elements respectively adopt the form of snakes or frogs, gather to conceive an egg from which the Sun will spring. When the cult of *Thoth* develops in **Khmun**, the theologians modify the initial beliefs: the primordial gods that formerly came out of nothingness, would as a matter of fact have been created by *Thoth.*

Here, in the capital of the 15th nome of Upper Egypt, *Thoth* reigns as master. This is why the town was called **Hermopolis** by the Greeks, in reference to the god *Hermes, Thoth*'s Hellenistic counterpart. The popularity of this god, often represented as a baboon or an ibis, dates back to a distant era. However, it owes its immense popularity to its unlimited powers rather than its origins. He teaches all sciences and possesses the entirety of the knowledge that can be spread. In order to manage this, he has invented a tool capable of transmitting this amount of knowledge: the scripture. Thus he is at the same time god of mathematics, letters and sciences; inventor of the calendar, the writing, the laws and the figures; and patron of scribes, astronomers, doctors, magicians and architects. *Hermes* also has a say in the underworld: he is the divine scribe *par excellence*, and fulfils the role of messenger. He introduces the deceased into the hall of judgement where *Osiris* and the forty two divinities of the funeral tribunal sit. At the time of the weighing of the soul, he notes down the verdict on sacred tablets.

Of the ancient town, set in a very fertile area, very little remains, as it served as a stone quarry during the nineteenth century. On the site, only a Christian basilica and a pylon of the *Ramesses* are visible. In the pylon around one thousand five hundred blocks were found which came from the temples of **Tell el-Amarna**, dismantled after the heresy of *Akhenaten*. From here, a seven-mile road, partially fitted along the Libyan cliff, leads to **Tuna el-Gebel** where one of the fourteen "Boundary Stelae" of **Akhetaten** and the necropolis of **el-Ashmunein** are found. For its part, the rock-cut stela marks the north west limit of the territory dedicated to the god *Aten*. It is one of the best preserved monuments of its kind. An inscription can be seen on it that recalls the foundation of the town; below it, a relief depicts *Akhenaten*, *Nefertiti* and two princesses worshipping the solar disk. As for the necropolis, it has several different areas. The first and most original one, consists of a series of catacombs in which mummies of baboons and of ibises, both animals sacred to *Thoth,* have been found by the hundreds. The second area comprises a building unique in its kind: the tomb of *Petosiris*, that dates back to the reign of *Philip Arrhidaeus*, the successor of *Alexander the Great*. Built in the form of a small temple with a vestibule and a chapel, it superbly exemplifies the merging of Greek and Egyptian styles. Lastly, the third area, which lies right to the south of the tomb of *Petosiris*, is a genuine city of the dead from the first centuries of our era. Including both tombs and stuccoed funerary buildings, its overall inspiration is Greek and its iconography Egyptian.

On the opposite bank at the foot of **Gebel el-Bersha**, a valley holds limestone quarries exploited in different eras and some rock tombs which are unfortunately very damaged. They belonged to the administration of the 15th nome of Upper Egypt, called the "Nome of the Hare", and date back to the 12th Dynasty. Only the tomb of *Thothotep*, "Superior Chief of the Principality of the Hare" from *Amenemhet II* to *Senusret III*, is worth mentioning. Despite its deterioration, it bears original scenes, both carved and painted. Notably on the west wall of the chapel, the deceased, followed by his family, assists in the transport of a colossal statue from the alabaster quarries of **Hatnub**. On the right side, common folk is depicted advancing from the gate of the temple to which the statue should be taken, towards the cortège in order to welcome it. A few miles to the north, the village of **el-Cheik'Ibada** occupies the place of the ancient **Antinoopolis**, which was totally devastated in the nineteenth century, when it furnished the materials necessary to build an important sugar refinery in the vicinity. The town was founded by *Hadrian* in the year 130 A.D. in memory of *Antinoos*, his favourite, drowned at this very spot. Survivors to the ravage are a theatre, two temples, two rows of colonnades, a hippodrome, a circus and a triumphal arch. Only the sketches drafted during the course of **Bonaparte**'s campaign in 1798 and published in volume IV of *The Description of Egypt*, allow us to appreciate the size of the ancient town.

In the place where the Nile makes a long loop towards the east, one can see in the distance, carved into the Arabian cliff, the **speos Artemidos**, a small rock-cut temple dedicated to the lion goddess *Pakhet* and built during the 18th Dynasty under the reign of the Queen **Hatshepsut,** as well as the tombs of **Beni Hasan**. On the western bank of the river, the small village of **Abu Qirqas** is the point of departure for a charming jaunt. Here, the river noticeably widens and assumes a particular character: the verdant islands and the floating islets of water lilies scattered across the river oblige the boatmen to navigate carefully to avoid these constant obstacles. This is without a shade of doubt the most pleasant journey that can be done on the Nile. Only the throbbing of the engine and the whistling of the wind disturbs its perfect plenitude. Sometimes, the cry of a wild duck or the taking off of a bird provokes a genuine storm of winged creatures which emerge panic-stricken from the thickets of tall grass and papyrus; then, after a second, everything becomes peaceful again. The stray boats float lazily in the current which in this part of the river is particularly gentle. Once the crossing is complete, the visitors are taken to the foot of the Arabian cliffs through a valley which, in width, barely reaches half a mile. A superb staircase built into the mountain provides access to the tombs of the "Princes of the Gazelle and of Monat Khufu". These are spread along the cliff face, on the same horizontal line, and linked by a rocky path that commands a perfect view over the entire Nile valley. In the middle, the river curls, dark, blue, imposing. It carves a passage through the cultivated lands that extend from either side of its banks. On the west side, a patchwork of many small cultivated areas stretches to the horizon while on the east side the meagre band of oases rapidly gives way to the desert, providing a brutal contrast between the dazzling green of the cultivated fields and the golden ochre of the sterile sands.

The necropolis of **Beni Hasan** includes thirty nine hypogea of unequal importance; only twelve of them are decorated, the rest are simple excavations which sometimes have interesting architectural structures. On the whole, they date from the beginning of the Middle Kingdom and evoke, with all the charm and purity which characterizes the period, the daily life and the funeral of the deceased. The lime-washed walls depict the work in the fields, the management of the cultivated areas, visits to the workshops, the hunt in the desert, the fishing in the marshes, the pilgrimage to **Abydos**, the funeral procession carrying the deceased to his final resting place… Moreover, certain tombs offer quite unusual scenes: these images, resembling comic strips, show wrestlers and athletes in the midst of acrobatic demonstrations. There are sometimes five or six levels of drawings where, two by two, the combatants fight with skill and ferocity.

The best moment to make the return journey is at sunset; the spectacle is then superb. Little by little, the cliff takes on various hues of tawny ochre and stands out against a slightly rose-tinted sky, while the valley displays a whole range of greens, lighter or darker depending on the type of crops. As for the river, it becomes green too,

A Ride on a Camel?

Numerous places in the valley offer traditional camel —actually dromedary— rides. It is a pleasant experience: one can, for example, travel from Giza to Saqqarah by the desert track rather than by the road, which allows no viewing of the Libyan range. Certainly, for the visitor unused to this peculiar mode of transportation the trip will seem a little uncomfortable and rough at the outset. Yet once the first few minutes have passed the hardness of the seat will be forgotten before the superb magnificence of the landscape.
Valley of the Nile,
Egypt.

and as the sun disappears, it gradually darkens into nothing more than a black and uniform mass. The journey to the north is accompanied by a slow and progressive transformation of the landscape of Middle Egypt. Between **el-Minya** and **Cairo**, the river constantly maintains its imposing look. Meanwhile the valley never ceases to widen, in particular westwards, sometimes

stretching more than 10 miles long. Here, naturally, agriculture is queen. The fields and prairies, richly irrigated by an ingenious system of channels, follow each other as far as the eye can see. Ever since the construction of the **Aswan** dam, the lands have been subjected to an intensive exploitation with the injection of water and the use of fertilizers to improve the harvests. The results have been encouraging since, in thirty years, production has doubled and certain lands which would formerly yield only one harvest a year now produce two or three. However, how strenuous is the **fellah**'s job, how arduous his struggle to extract the most out of the land! The word **"fellah"** designates the Egyptian peasant, whose way of life and work has remained unchanged since ancient times.

Seeing him toil the earth from sunrise to sunset, one understands the derision in *Herodotus*'s tableau: *"True, these are the men who nowadays make less effort in earning their harvests... When the river comes of its own accord to water the fields and then retires, its task done, everyone sows his land and lets out his pigs. As they tread the soil, the animals bury the grain with their hooves; the man then doesn't have to do but wait for the time of harvest and, once the pigs have stomped on the tweeds, collect the grain."* In reality, the life of the **fellah** is not that easy. From the beginning of times Egypt has owed its resources to the relentless labour of the **fellah** who tirelessly works a land that does not belong to him, and provides sustenance for a population that in exchange hardly gives him enough to subsist. Things have evolved very little over the centuries, but the government is determined to modify the situation. An analysis of the farming scenes depicted on the walls of civil tombs of the ancient era shows that the same techniques, the same tools, the same systems of irrigation endure after four or five thousand years. In effect, the two most commonly used hydraulic instruments in Egypt are still the **chaduf**, a seesaw-like implement that permits the easy extraction of water, and the **noria**, a large waterwheel with many clay pots that raises water. Originally, this machine was made of wood and was turned by a draught animal; in most of the large exploitations along the Nile, wood has nowadays given way to metal and the animal has been replaced by an engine or an electric pump.

Similarly, the life and the habits of the **fellah** have seen few modifications. Often, he lives modestly, as testify his clothes, his diet, and his house. He lives in a village where, like him, his friends and neighbours have cultivated the soil for generations. His house is made of mud brick or clay, topped by a roof of straw, and very often shelters a very large family. In effect, the **fellah** always has many children, and has done so since the time of the Pharaohs; they must protect him and aid him as he has no one else. This family is his reason to live and its only support; he is content and seems happy. In any case, he never complains, which is one of the **fellah**'s greatest strengths. Like most Egyptians from the country, he wears the traditional clothing, the **galabieh,** a long and ample robe, generally made from plain cotton. As for the woman, she wears a long robe streaked with bright colours on which she places a black shawl while a scarf, the **melayeh,** covers her hair. It is rare to see country women still wearing a veil, undoubtedly for reasons of comfort, but also because the tradition is waning.

Their diet, quite rudimentary, lacks variety: **foul** (large boiled red beans), lentils, onions, grilled corn, vinegar-soaked vegetables, fried peppers, rice, salted cheese, bread and dates. In short, lots of carbohydratres, few fresh vegetables, and no meat or poultry, unless it is a holiday where one consumes **gamus**, a type of Indian buffalo, camel, chicken or duck. To accompany a meal, the **fellah** drinks very sweet black tea or water which he gets from one of several jars scattered around the village, since running water remains a luxury which most houses do not have. The same applies to electricity; despite the enormous effort to electrify Egypt after the construction of the **Aswan** dam, certain hamlets have not received their installations and still live by the light of kerosene lamps and candles.

On the road which separates **Tell el-Amarna** from **Cairo,** numerous small villages, all identical, are scattered along the eastern bank. Initially separated from each other by several hundred feet, they progressively become an inhabited continuum as one approaches **Fayum,** the beginning of Lower Egypt. For more than half a century, Egypt has suffered from a serious demographic problem: 2 million inhabitants in 1800, 6 million in 1900, 20 million in 1950, 38 million in 1976 and more than 60 million today. However, even more worrying is the fact that the country increases by 1.2 to 1.5 million inhabitants a year. Moreover, to feed and house this population, only 4% of the total area of Egypt is nowadays susceptible of exploitation, around 25,000 square miles. Aware of this serious demographic problem, the government, notably since *Sadat*, has sought to curb the birth rate, which remains too high, especially in the countryside. However, weighty traditions —ancestral, religious, familiar— radically oppose any birth control measures. Thus, three to four thousand children are born every day to parents who do not know whether they will be able to feed their kids even a mere frugal meal a day. Often, several generations of the same family live crammed in a single house. Moreover, the demographic boom is such that it inevitably leads to the building of more and more dwellings.

Resting on the Banks of the Nile

In the countryside, young Egyptian girls are always dressed in long dresses of bright colours and cover their hair with a small scarf. Their appearance allows one to distinguish them from married women who normally wear less colourful clothing and are wrapped in a traditional melayeh, a type of large black shawl. Here, with big aluminium pots or jars of baked clay, the young girls have come to draw water from the Nile, which they use for washing, cleaning or small daily chores. Carrying the pots on their heads, they go their separate ways after having taken advantage for a moment of the freshness of the river.
Banks of the Nile, Egypt.

The logic of the process is quite a simple one: each new building enlarges the village; each new village encroaches on cultivated land. In fact, there remains no place that has not been developed along the Valley of the Nile. The population density has reached levels that are almost beyond belief: almost 2,000 inhabitants per square mile by 152 in France. Needless to say, this over-population implies serious economic problems: massive imports of necessities (more than 50% of the consumed foodstuffs are brought from abroad), trade deficit, increasing debt, a drop in the standard of living, unemployment, illiteracy… Furthermore, Egypt suffers from a lack of educational infrastructure. In the countryside, the **fellahs** and craftsmen do not know how to read or write since, for various reasons, most have never been to school. On the one hand, there is a lack of schools, and schooling is costly for most families. On the other hand, not only does a child in school represent a considerable cost, but, more importantly, he is not making any money. Nowadays, in certain families, all the income, whatever its source, is necessary to feed the household. Quite often, small chores are passed from father to son, and from the age of seven or eight, the boy will help the father in his work. As for the girls, they stay at home to help their mother in performing certain household tasks. In large centres, where the standard of living is much higher, the abundance of adolescents obliges educational institutions to choose their students: according to the latest estimations 54% of the population is less than twenty years old and 36%, less than twelve. On their own, these figures explain why the Egyptian government is experiencing difficulties in fulfilling this need; it is not fifty or a hundred schools that must be built, but thousands. Money makes all the difference; the establishments capable of providing a good education are filled with the children of high officials and wealthy businessmen. At the same time, public schools receive, in their bursting classrooms, less fortunate children who receive an education that is poorly adapted to the new demands of the country.

Despite this very alarming situation, Middle Egypt has developed, at the cost of great efforts and constant sacrifices, numerous and important settlements. By way of example, **Beni Suef**, county town of the province of the same name, remains one of the most active economic and industrial centres of the region. Furthermore, agriculture prospers here because the valley reaches it greatest length between the Nile and the Libyan desert, 11 miles of crops and varied fruit trees. The town is found at a crossroads, serving the four corners of the country: **Cairo**, **Aswan**, **Ras Zafarana** and, finally, **Fayum**.

Fayum

Fayum is the name given to the region situated in the Libyan desert, about 69 miles south west from **Cairo**. From **Beni Suef**, from **Cairo** or the intermediary villages, roads, trails and railway lines lead to the heart of this depression, remarkable for its size, its water supplies and its richness. This oasis, if one is allowed to qualify **Fayum** as such, forms a gigantic circle of 38 miles in diameter linked to the Nile by **Bahr Yussef**, the "River of Joseph." This small river separates from **Ibrahimeh Canal** at the city of **Dairut**, located south of **Tell el-Amarna**, and then flows parallel to the Nile until **Beni Suef** where it briefly turns off towards the west to take the route of **Fayum**. From there, it loses all its vigour and ramifies into several branches which gradually become narrower until they disappear into the surrounding land. Of them all, only two streams of **Bahr Yussef** effectively arrive at the bottom of the depression marked by **Birket Qarun**, quondam **Lake Moeris**. A legend explains the origins of this lake: it was dug at the command of Pharaoh *Moeris* who, furthermore, would have had two pyramids, and their respective royal colossi, built in the middle of the lake. Scientists have successfully proved the lake to be a natural one, yet it can be easily understood how a legend could arise in ancient times that accounted for this inland sea lost in the middle of the desert. Due to its gradual subsiding, **Lake Qarun** is about 28 feet below sea level. It scarcely covers a fifth of **Fayum**'s area whereas in the ancient era it was much larger and would have certainly covered the greatest part of the oasis. This is the reason for which the ancient Egyptians called this land **To-Che**, the "Country of the Lake", and the Copts, **Phiom**, "The Lake".

From the beginning of the Pharaonic period, the inhabitants of the Nile valley became interested in this region which, like other oases of the western desert, they found to be a completely unexpected reserve of raw materials and farming products. It is the kings of the Middle Kingdom who first attached any value

to **Fayum**. Under *Amenemhet III*, unarguably *Herodo-tus*'s *Moeris*, irrigation channels are dug, impounding barriers are laid out, and protective dikes are constructed to dry out the flooded areas. Somewhat neglected by the kings of the 18th Dynasty, the region develops again under the reign of *Ramesses II*, who has it settled with entire colonies of farmers, labourers, and Nubian and Asian workers.

Meanwhile, the real expansion of **Fayum** coincides with the arrival of the Greeks in Egypt. The Ptolemaic sovereigns have Greek and Macedonian tenants assume the control of the region's large farms with the goal of exploiting this vast area to the full. They must have been successful, since Greek visitors marvelled at the abundance and the variety of **Fayum**'s crops: citrus fruits, mangoes, vegetables, cereals, olives, and all types of flowers which still today lend the region their colourful appearance. The accounts also speak of the exceptional integration of the Greek colonists. In less than fifty years, the Hellenistics customs, language and divinities disappear from the oasis, giving way to a culture directly descended from the Pharaonic heritage. They entrust their dead to *Osiris*, worship *Sobek*, dress in the Egyptian fashion, and quickly they forget that the first colonists were of pure Greek blood.

The heart of the oasis is **Medinet el-Fayum**, a town built on the ruins of the ancient **Shedit**, the **Crocodilopolis** of the Greeks. This name refers to the crocodile *Sobek*, considered in the whole region as the universal master and the divine creator. His essential role is to fight against the enemies of *Ra*, the sun, these being principally fish. At the same time, he protects men from the attacks of beasts and the hostile powers that reign in the marshes and waters of the Nile. Of the temple of *Sobek,* located at the north of the ancient town, virtually nothing remains; it vanished under two different onslaughts: first, the **sebakh** searchers; later, the enlargement of the modern town which has greatly encroached on the site. In all probability, this building dates back to the Middle Kingdom even if the last vestiges of its construction are limited to the pillars bearing the name of *Amenemhet III*. It was revamped by *Ramesses II*, as witnessed by certain fragments of blocks carrying his cartouche, and by the *Ptolemies*. Aside from this few scattered stones, the remains of a basin reserved for the sacred crocodiles can be descried. This type of cult, very developed along the Nile valley, rests on the idea that every animal is a repository of the divine power, hence the need to honour it and sustain it. The sacred animal is the visible manifestation of the divinity it represents. It may also be considered as a "living

The Nile

Generally, in the cities and towns located on the banks of the Nile, everything is planned so that the passer-by may enjoy the freshness of the river. Sometimes, there is a simple shaded corniche or promenade provided with benches where the locals come to chat and to unwind, especially after nightfall. Sometimes, gardens are laid out along the Nile; they provide a relaxed atmosphere which everyone relishes. The town of el-Minya boasts the finest banks to be seen in Middle Egypt. The Arabian range provides the background; the river, very wide at this point, flows in the middle; and in the foreground, pleasant little gardens spread along the bank.
Banks of the Nile,
el-Minya, Middle Egypt.

87

image of the cult", something that can be easily grasped by the faithful. In **Fayum**, the crocodile is held as sacred; according to *Herodotus*, *"each region chooses a crocodile and feeds it"*. The following excerpt elaborates on the maintenance of the beast: *"once tamed, they place beads of molten glass or gold in its ears and bracelets on the front legs. Alive, they offer it special food and lavish attention upon it; dead, they embalm it and deposit it in a sacred sepulchre."*

Some 20 miles separates **Beni Suef** from **Medinet el-Fayum**, which indicates the extent to which the oasis spreads along the banks of the Nile. This extreme proximity undoubtedly explains the particular interest shown by the ancient Egyptians in the region, at a time when distance presented a much greater handicap than today. In a mere half an hour, private or collective taxis and buses take passengers from one place to another; however, for the visitor, it is preferable to use private transportation in view of the many not-to-be-missed tourist locations along the way. In fact, **Fayum**'s Fathers, the kings of the 12th Dynasty, decided to establish their last residence on this main route near the administrative capital of **el-Lisht**, thirty miles to the north. Initially, *Senusret II* built a pyramid of brick at **Illahun**. Unfortunately very deteriorated today, it was originally coated with limestone and provided with many rooms, chambers and passageways anarchically arranged around the sepulchre. To the south of the pyramid, the shafts of the tomb of *Sithathoriunet*, princess of royal blood, revealed an important quantity of jewels of exceptional craftsmanship.

Later, *Amenemhet III* chose to build his funeral complex on the site of **Hawara**, very close to the heart of **Fayum**, since the ancient town of **Shedit** was merely a few miles away. Much more than the pyramid, equally deteriorated, it is above all the funerary temple which possesses an exceptional character. It has been identified as the famous **"Labyrinth"** referred to by Greek visitors. If one believes *Herodotus*, these were the temple's characteristics in the fifth century B.C.: *"A labyrinth was built up Lake Moeris, near the town called Crocodilopolis. I could see with my own eyes that this building surpassed all that was said. If one were to assemble all the walls and constructions made by the Greeks, the resulting whole would be inferior in both effort and cost to this*

labyrinth (...) It is composed of twelve covered courtyards whose doors are arranged in two opposing rows, six doors facing the north and six facing the south. One surrounding wall encloses everything. In the interior one finds two kinds of rooms; one subterranean, the other built above ground on top of the former: there are three thousand of these rooms, one thousand five hundred for each kind. We ourselves saw and walked the upper rooms, thus we speak for ourselves. As for the inferior rooms, we only know them by hearsay, because the Egyptians in charge of guarding them absolutely refused to show them to us; they say they contained the tombs of the kings who built this place as well as those of sacred crocodiles."

In our days, the temple consists of a few vestiges and its traces are difficult to find. A little north of this funeral complex extends the civil necropolis used over the eras by high officials of the oasis. Certain tombs revealed amazing collections of portraits dating back to the first four centuries of our era and covering the whole of the Roman domination. Nearly a thousand objects of this type have been found in Egypt; irrespective of their place of discovery, they all are referred to as "portraits of **Fayum**", for on the whole they tend to come from this region. Painted in tempera or in wax, either hot or cold, over wood or canvas, these portraits were placed on the head of the mummy and kept there with bandages. Is this perhaps the final stage in the evolution of the Egyptian funeral mask? At any rate, it attests the successful survival of many Pharaonic traditions well after the extinction of this civilization.

Nevertheless, **Fayum** remains above all an oasis. Besides these precious archaeological remains, one must not forget to admire the enchanting landscapes that the region offer. To the west, **Fayum** opens to the **Sahara** where everything is beauty and immensity. The spectacle is as unusual as it is admirable. As far as the eye can see, there are high dunes, smooth and uniform, deserts of sand or coloured stones, and high limestone plateaux of immaculate whiteness. At the heart of the oasis, the orchards, the vegetables and the crops reveal a range of different colours where green, yellow and red reign and blend with the tones of the neighbouring desert. Here and there, villages or simple hamlets display the sparkling colours of Egypt.

The Date Palm

Numerous palm groves lie along the Nile valley which surround the different oases, notably those of the Libyan Desert. The date palm, often represented in tombs dating from the Pharaohs' era, is Egypt's ubiquitous tree. It measures dozens of feet in height and produces large red dates that can be eaten in two ways: dried, as in western countries, or fresh, as in Egypt.
Nile valley,
Egypt.

THE NORTH,
THE LOWER EGYPT

From the Fayum region to the Mediterranean

Several routes leave **Fayum**. The southern route leads to **Beni Suef** and allows to reach Upper Egypt or the ports of the Red Sea easily, particularly **Ras Zafarana** on the **Gulf of Suez**. The northern route runs across the Libyan Desert and leads directly to **Cairo** by the plateau of **Giza**. The two intermediary roads join the Nile 17.5 miles north of **Beni Suef** and offer the visitor the chance to follow the famous "route the of the pyramids" from **Maidum** to **Giza**. On this trail, there are more than thirty pyramids in reasonable condition rising majestically along the western bank of the Nile which belonged to the sovereigns of the Ancient and Middle Kingdom. The idea of being buried in a pyramid goes back to *Djoser,* the first Pharaoh of the 3rd Dynasty, and to his architect of genius, *Imhotep*, deified in the Late Period for his wisdom and his talents in healing. From the beginning of the Old Kingdom, the theologians chose as a primary cult that of the creator, the solar god *Ra*. Since it is the commoners' fate to revive uniquely in their tombs, where they enjoy a second existence, the sovereign seeks to become solar energy itself: after his death, he will join his father, the Sun, and become one with him.

The **"Pyramid texts"** suggest several ways of rising to heaven, notably the stairway and the solar rays. The pyramid can therefore be interpreted as the symbolic representation of this ladder to the sun, a theory which seems confirmed by certain funerary texts: *"the ladder is installed for me to see the gods"*. Thus, the step pyramid represents the stairway and the perfect pyramid symbolizes the petrified sun rays. Whether Pharaoh chose one sepulchre or the other, the vocation of the edifice remains the same: to enable the traffic between Heaven and Earth so that the sovereign can profit from the offerings deposited at his funerary temple.

Not all of the listed pyramids hold the same interest for the visitor; some are in a perfect condition (*Djoser, Sneferu, Khufu, Khafra* or *Menkaura*), while some others resemble a mound of fallen rocks (*Sahura, Neferirkara, Nyuserra* or *Unas*), a shapeless mass of raw brick (*Senusret II, Senusret III* or *Amenemhet III*), or an enormous excavation, notably at **Zawiet el-Aryan**, where the owner remains unknown, and at **Abu Rawach** (*Djedefra*). Upon leaving the oasis of **Fayum**, the profile of the pyramid stands si houetted against the horizon: it announces the site of **Maidum**, point of departure for the "route of the pyramids".

The "Route of the Pyramids"

The exact dating of the pyramid of **Maidum** still poses a problem. It is generally attributed to *Sneferu*, the founder of the 4tg Dynasty; however, he already possesses two pyramids in **Dahshur**, and the probability that he owned three is minimal. Thus it would be logical to think that this monument belongs to his father, the king *Huni*, who would have started the construction while his son was only responsible for completing it. Whatever the case, this building, called the "False Pyramid", is very interesting to study because it marks a decisive turning point in the evolution of pyramidal tombs and funerary complexes. The edifice combines features from both the step pyramid, like that of *Djoser*, and the true pyramid, like *Khufu*'s. Initially, the plan was to construct a seven-terraced edifice on which a six-stepped portion of masonry would be imposed. The initial project was modified, apparently twice, until it became an eight-stepped structure measuring 322 feet high and filled in with limestone to acquire the look of a real pyramid.

Unfortunately, certain faults in the conception and construction led to the partial collapse of the pyramid; this explains its present-day appearance. At its feet spreads a vast necropolis of **mastabas**: this name, meaning "bench" in Arabic, refers to the nonroyal tombs of the Old Kingdom. The **mastaba** is composed of a superstructure, the funerary chapel and the **serdab**, and an infrastructure, the shaft and the burial chamber. The tomb is entered by the funerary chapel, the only part that can be freely accessed. It is here that those closest to the deceased came to leave flowers, make offerings of water and burn incense. The deceased is in permanent contact with the world of the living through a stele created as a false door. On the walls are depicted scenes of the daily life of the deceased, since, according to the beliefs of the Ancient Kingdom, life after death is but a continuation of earthly life. Thus, the representations, animated by the image's creative power, will permit the deceased to lead, in the underworld, an identical existence to the one he enjoyed on earth. The **serdab**, a small room designed to shelter the statue of the deceased, closed on all sides and devoid of any décor, is connected to the chapel by a slot made at eye height; this feature permitted the owner of the tomb to enjoy the prayers and the offerings addressed to him. The shafts, generally very deep in order to

avoid any profanation, give access to the burial chamber which contains the mummified corpse inside a sarcophagus and other funeral objects. After the funeral this chamber is sealed with a heavy granite portcullis, and the shafts are filled in with earth and stones.

In **Maidum,** one of the **mastabas** revealed two statues, exceptional for their quality and their excellent condition, depicting Prince *Rahotep* and *Nofret,* his consort, both characters belonging to the royal entourage. *Daninos,* the discoverer, tells how, at the time of the clearing of the tomb, the workman in charge of exploring the passageway with a candle panicked because *"he found himself in the presence of two living heads whose staring eyes filled him with such terror that he believed he would never find the exit again."* The surprising stare is believed to come from the embedded eyes which give the statue the illusion of life. *Daninos* himself explains the technique used by the craftsmen: *"An encasing of bronze, representing the eyelids, embeds a globe of white quartz deftly veined with red, in the centre of which a slightly rounded piece of rock crystal represents the pupil. Under this crystal a brilliant pebble is fixed which determines the point of sight and produces this radiance which can be mistaken as a sign of persisting life."*

The "False Pyramid"
Situated to the north west of Fayum, the pyramid of Maidum bears witness to the difficulties encountered by the Ancient Egyptians when erecting a real pyramid. In all probability, it was begun by Huni, the last sovereign of the 3rd Dynasty, and finished by his son and successor, Sneferu. In reality, this edifice constitutes a middle phase between two types of buildings: the step pyramid (like that of Djoser) and a real pyramid (like that of Khufu). However, at a date still disputed, the pyramid partially collapsed: was it a construction flaw, a weakness of the structure, an error in conception? These are not easy questions. Nevertheless, whatever the problem, truth is it was quickly resolved, for the "Red Pyramid" of Sneferu at Dahshur, built slightly later, is a genuine pyramid.
Pyramid of Huni/Sneferu,
Old Kingdom,
Maidum, Lower Egypt.

The Pyramid of Djoser
North Saqqara
Present name: The Step Pyramid
First Pharaoh of the 3rd Dynasty
Most ancient pyramid in Egypt
Built by Imhotep
Base: 397 x 358 feet
Original height: 197 feet
Present height: 190 feet

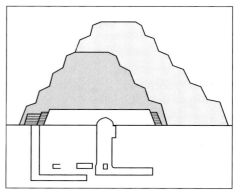

The First Pyramid of Sneferu
Dahshur
Original Name: "The Southern Shining Pyramid"
Present name: The Rhomboidal Pyramid
First Pharaoh of the 4th Dynasty
Attempt at true pyramid
Base: 602 x 602 feet
Original height: 344 feet
Present height: 318 feet
Slope: 54º27 (lower half), 43º22 (upper half)

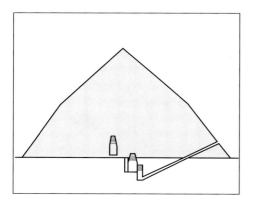

The Pyramid of Khufu
Giza
Original name: "Khufu's Horizon"
Present name: "The Great Pyamid of Giza"
Second Pharaoh of the 4th dynasty
True pyramid; First Wonder of the World
Base: 755 x 755 feet
Original height: 419 feet
Present height: 449 feet
Slope: 51º50

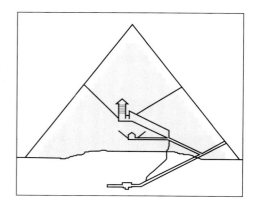

The Pyramid of Huni

Maidum
Original name: "Stable is Sneferu"
Present name: "The False Pyramid"
Last Pharaoh of the 3rd Dynasty
Completed by his son Sneferu
Step Pyramid
Base: 472 x 472 feet
Original height: 307 feet
Present height: 213 feet

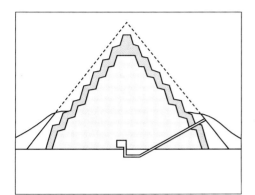

The Second Pyramid of Sneferu

Dahshur
Original name: "The Shining Pyramid"
Present name: "The Red Pyramid"
First Pharaoh of the 4th Dynasty
True pyramid
Base: 722 x 722 feet
Original height: 341 feet
Present height: 325 feet
Slope: 43°22

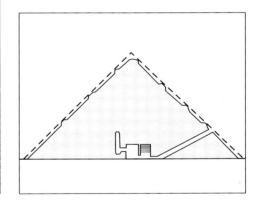

The Pyramid of Khafra

Giza
Name: "Great is Khafra"
Original name: "The Second Pyramid of Giza"
Fourth Pharaoh of the 4th Dynasty
True pyramid
Base: 707 x 707 feet
Original height: 471 feet
Present height: 448 feet
Slope: 53°70

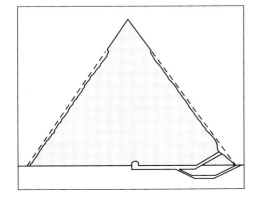

After the site of **Maidum**, the **Fayum** road definitively meets the Nile Valley and does not leave it until **Cairo**. From then on, the strip of arable land stretching along the river gets narrower, so much so that sometimes hardly 2 to 2.5 miles separate the Nile from the desert where the Pharaohs' eternal resting places lie. Here, the valley offers the image of an Egypt overpopulated and where every square inch is used. The dwellings and the crops follow one another, or even entangle together without any logic. In the heart of the hastily improvised markets by the road, women dressed in long colourful robes wander from stall to stall. They stop, argue, buy, place their heavy loads on their heads and end up swallowed by swarming crowds that exude the joy of living. The men, when they are not working in the fields, lounge on the terrace of a cafe where they talk and smoke their **narguiles**, a type of water pipe in which the tobacco is mixed with honey, giving off a sweet and pungent odour. Further on, beyond the enclosure formed by the palm groves, stand the pyramids. One first notices those of **el-Lisht** that belonged, the first to *Amenemhet I*, and the second, to *Senusret I*, Pharaohs of the 12th Dynasty. They are very deteriorated and do not hold any real interest for the visitor, who anyway is not permitted to enter due to serious infiltrations of water from the phreatic layer.

Some 20 miles away, lies the site of **Dahshur**, established by *Sneferu*, who here possesses two sepulchres: the "Rhomboidal Pyramid" and the "Red Pyramid." The oldest, called rhomboidal because of its unusual shape, stands to the south; halfway up, its slope drops by more than ten degrees for reasons which have yet to be adequately explained. Certain Egyptologists attribute this to the premature death of the king: the works had to be accelerated in order to bury *Sneferu* in his pyramid as it is the only one that, with certainty, can be attributed to him. As a matter of fact, the initiative saved very little work since it hardly changed the final volume of the structure: the question of time therefore cannot seriously be considered. Other specialists think that the collapse of the **Maidum** pyramid is the cause of this peculiarity: realising their lack of expertise, the architects preferred to abandon the construction of a true pyramid in order to prevent any contingency. However, the pyramid of **Maidum** does not seem to have collapsed during construction but rather during the New Kingdom. A final thesis tends to blame the problems that appeared

during the building of the high vaulted chambers. Whichever the case, to this day no document has been produced that confirms any of these suppositions. With the "Red Pyramid", the Egyptian architects reached their long desired goal: to build a genuine pyramid. However, a detailed analysis of the dimensions shows that certain technical constraints could not be resolved: the inclination adopted is ten degrees lower than that of *Khufu*. Thus, on more or less equal bases, 770 feet for *Sneferu* and 805 feet for *Khufu*, the "Red Pyramid" is 140 feet lower in elevation. The building therefore appears more firmly seated but less pointed and more massive. The ruins of the three other pyramids lie on the eastern part of the plateau. To the south stands the so called "Black Pyramid", *Amenemhet III*'s cenotaph, his real tomb being located in **Fayum** at **Hawara**. Today, the monument looks like a mass of mud bricks as the fine limestone facing which covered it disappeared long ago.

Further on, a few scattered blocks indicate the presence of a building: these are the remains of the stone pyramid of *Amenemhet II*.

To the North, stands another pyramid in mud brick, the most imposing of the 12th Dynasty: it belonged to *Senusret III*. Amongst these last two monuments, *Jacques de Morgan* unearthed the tombs of princesses and queens of the Middle Kingdom. Incredible jewellery of gold and precious stones was found; especially in the tombs of *Mereret*, wife of *Senusret III*, and that of *Khnumet*, daughter of *Amenemhet II*; these pieces are conserved in the **Egyptian Museum of Cairo**.

Scarcely a mile separates **Dahshur** from **Saqqara**. Often, people who venture to **Dahshur** coming from **Saqqara**, do so by the desert, either on camel or horseback or, those brave enough, on foot. However, a proper visit to both sites on one day is impossible, because of the size of the necropolis of **Saqqara** which extends over 5.5 square miles. It is true that most of the area is not covered in ancient monuments, but the distances that separate the different groups are restricting and time consuming. **Saqqara** is without doubt one of the most touristic places in the country. It is formed by a vast complex of buildings, the most ancient dating back to the 1st Dynasty and the most recent to Coptic Egypt: tombs of the Thinite era, pyramids and **mastabas** of the Old Kingdom, tombs and chapels of the New Kingdom, caves from the Late Period, Greco-Roman sepulchres, necropolis of

sacred animals… Strangely, one must wait until the middle of the nineteenth century to see the rebirth of this cyclopean "city of the dead". The impulse was given by *Auguste Mariette*, a Frenchman who, in 1851 discovered a subterranean necropolis reserved for sacred bulls: the **Serapeum**. Immediately, hundreds of Egyptologists of all kinds flocked to **Saqqara**. Some were lucky to make splendid discoveries; others worked on still visible structures. However, all of them helped to broaden the field of knowledge about Ancient Egypt.

Generally, the visitors who come to **Saqqara** are unaware of the true richness of the site, dominated by the funeral complex of *Djoser*, founder of the 3rd Dynasty. The excavations and analysis of the structures, entrusted to *Jean-Philippe Lauer* after 1926, allowed the reconstruction of various elements of this vast complex which mark a radical turning point in architecture. Two innovations characterize the site: the use of stone for monumental purposes and the adoption of the pyramid as a funeral structure. The idea comes from *Imhotep*, architect of

Djoser. At the heart of an esplanade marked by an enclosure, he conceived a step pyramid surrounded by halls, cult chapels, courtyards and the ceremonial buildings intended to ensure the passage of the king's soul to the underworld. The pyramid bears traces of several modifications: initially, *Imhotep* imagined a **mastaba** connected to a burial chamber via several shafts; later on, the building was enlarged to the east and converted into a four-stepped structure; finally, two more terraces were added that gave the building the aspect of a six-stepped pyramid over 200 feet in height. Numerous stone vases have been unearthed, many of them belonging to *Djoser*, but others bearing the names of his predecessors: is this an act of royal piety intended to preserve the funerary objects of those Pharaohs? In the passageway, a mummified left foot was exhumed: was it the only vestige of *Djoser*'s mummy? Despite the remarkable work of *Jean-Philippe Lauer* and his team, many questions remain unanswered to this day.

South east of the enclosure of *Djoser*, the Egyptologist *Zakaria Gonein* discovered, in 1950, a very similar

The Hunt in the Marshes

The mastabas which surround the pyramids represent, on certain parts of the tombs, scenes of daily life. The images often depict hunting or fishing parties on the Nile or in the marshes. The mastaba of Mereruka, priest of the pyramid of the 6th Dynasty king Teti, boasts a remarkable example of this type of representation. An ichneumon, a kind of mongoose, can be seen standing on the stem of a lotus flower; it is about to assault a nest of kingfishers sheltering three chicks whose panic-stricken parents are trying to protect.
Mastabal of Mereruka,
Old Kingdom,
Saqqara, Lower Egypt.

funeral complex, that of Pharaoh *Sekhemkhet*, *Djoser*'s direct successor. However, the pyramid was left unfinished, may be because of the premature death of the king, and vanished beneath the sands. Between these two complexes, of imposing size, lies the pyramid of *Unas*, the last sovereign of the 5th Dynasty whose funeral structure extends to the east, that is, towards the Nile. It is composed of several elements. The valley temple, situated on the edge of the desert, receives the remains of the deceased at the time of the funeral; it is the place of welcome and purification, the unavoidable, necessary gateway for the dead into his tomb. From this sanctuary an uphill causeway, covered and decorated, leads to the funerary temple built on the east face of the pyramid. Here is where the royal statues were worshipped and the offerings made that would ensure the sovereign's afterlife. Lastly, there stands the pyramid, the king's tomb. From the outside, *Unas*'s pyramid does not hold much interest as it is partly collapsed. Conversely, a visit to the interior allows one to discover, in the antechamber and in the room of the sarcophagus, a series of texts engraved on the walls: the so called **"Pyramid Texts"**.

Initially, the pyramids were anepigraphic; only the proprietor's cartouches would appear here and there. From the reign of *Unas* until the end of the 6th Dynasty, all royal pyramids contained a version, more or less complete, of these texts. They consist of a series of formulas meant to guarantee the passage of the soul to the hereafter. The magical incantations provided the deceased with all that was necessary for the purification of the soul, the overcoming of obstacles and the survival. Their power resides in the magical effect of the spoken and written word by way of the recitation of these formulas on the day of the funeral, and their subsequent inscription on the walls of the chamber. Four hundred formulas have been discovered, although no pyramid possesses all of them: some have formulas that are missing in others. To the west of *Djoser*'s complex stand the ruins of *Userkaf*'s and *Teti*'s pyramids, respective founders of the 5th and 6th Dynasties.

On either side of this group of royal tombs, high officials constructed their eternal resting places. Right at the foot of the pyramids are the **mastabas** of the 5th and 6th Dynasties, some of which feature amongst the greatest treasures of Egyptian art. The most remarkable ones stand along the pyramid of *Teti*; they exemplify how the superstructure of the **mastaba**, originally consisting of a chapel and a **serdab**, evolved over the course of the Old Kingdom. That of his vizier, *Mera* or *Mereruka*, stretches over 140 feet. It comprises not less than thirty rooms, built to serve the funeral cults of the vizier, his spouse, *Sesheshet*, and his son, *Meri-Teti*.

Apart from the numerous tombs contemporary of the pyramids and known as **mastabas**, this part of the plateau holds many tombs of the New Kingdom, the most famous of which being that of *Horemheb*, last Pharaoh of the 18th Dynasty. Actually, *Horemheb* possessed two tombs: one in the **Valley of the Kings**, and the other at **Saqqara**. This is explained by the fact that before becoming King of Egypt, *Horemheb* was the commander in chief of the army under the reigns of *Akhenaten*, *Tutankhamun* and the God's Father *Ay*. Thus, like all high officials of the era he had a tomb built at **Saqqara**; when he became Pharaoh, he left the civil necropolis for the royal necropolis. He had a hypogeum carved in **West Thebes**, in the **Valley of the Kings**. His tomb at **Saqqara** was exposed in the nineteenth century; its statues and reliefs were thoroughly plundered and it afterwards fell into oblivion until its re-discovery in 1975. The excavations have determined that this tomb, remarkable for the quality of its execution, was used by the queen *Mutnedjemet*, one of *Horemheb*'s wives. The west of the plateau is served by a road that goes to the north of the *Djoser* complex and allows one to return to the **Serapeum**, the necropolis of the sacred bulls. It consists of a series of subterranean galleries opening onto sepulchral chambers designed to receive, in their enormous granite or basalt coffins, the mummies of sacred animals. The **Serapeum** consists of three groups of tombs corresponding to three periods of burial: to the south, the isolated tombs of the bulls buried between the reign of *Amenhotep III* and the thirtieth year of the reign of *Ramesses II*; in the centre, "the small subterranean passages" of the *Apis* buried between the thirtieth year of *Ramesses II* and the twentieth year of *Psamtek I*, the first sovereign of the 26th Dynasty; to the north, the "great subterranean passages" used from the fifty second year of *Psamtek I* to the end of the Greek era. However, only a part of this necropolis is open to the public. The isolated tombs have disappeared beneath the sands and the "small passages" have been closed since their discovery: actually only the latest catacombs are visible. A corridor 690 feet long opens on

either side to sepulchral chambers containing coffins of black granite of astonishing dimensions: 14 feet long, 8.5 feet wide and over 10 feet high. Twenty four sarcophagi of this type were discovered, although they had been looted long before.

This part of the plateau, dominated by the *Djoser* complex, forms the necropolis of **North Saqqara**. Generally, visitors do not have the opportunity to go beyond its limits. However, in the distance, two groups of pyramids can be seen: to the south, the site of **South Saqqara**, occupied by the Pharaohs of the 6th Dynasty; to the north, that of **Abusir**, reserved for the sovereigns of the 5th Dynasty. Both are quite deteriorated and very often only those who travel by camel or on horseback to **Giza** or **Dahshur** stop at these two necropolis. The arrival at **Giza** through the desert offers one of the most dazzling spectacles one can wish for: at first the pyramid of *Menkaura* appears with its three small satellite pyramids; next, the pyramid of *Khafra*, and finally, that of *Khufu*, the First Wonder of the World.

It is *Khufu*, son of the king *Sneferu* and the queen *Hetepheres*, who inaugurates the plateau of **Giza**. Tapping into the conceptions pioneered by his father at **Dahshur**,

Khufu fancies a pyramid which constitutes a genuine technical feat: the angle of its faces is 52°; whereas *Sneferu*'s was only 44°. The result is startling: the building, very pointed, seems to touch the sky, a goal often sought by the builders of pyramids. The monument consists of two million three hundred thousand blocks and covers an area of 185,000 square feet; within its actual dimensions it measures 805 feet a side and 480 feet in height. At that time, the **Tura** limestone facing which covered the pyramid, torn down during the Arab period, brought its total height up to 511 feet. Thus, until the nineteenth century, the architect of the pyramid of *Khufu* held a world record: it remained the tallest building in the world for four thousand five hundred years. Numerous archaeologists have a fondness for this mysterious pyramid. They would love to determine the techniques used for its construction. Unfortunately, the problem remains unsolved because no historical document has appeared to confirm any of the theories advanced by researchers; all that exist are hypotheses, some more plausible than others. Regarding the internal plan of the structure, it reveals at least three successive stages: a subterranean chamber, a project that was abandoned before being completed; the so-called "Queen's Chamber", within the body of the stonework, but equally abandoned

Jousting on the Waters
This 6th Dynasty mastaba is divided into two distinct areas: one part is reserved for Akhuthotep and the other for his son, Ptahhotep. The most beautiful scenes of the sepulchre decorate the walls of Ptahhotep's chapel: they are regarded as masterpieces of the bas-relief sculpture of the Old Kingdom. The back wall of the chapel shows the deceased contemplating different scenes from daily life; one of these recounts a joust on the Nile in which many boats take part, the spear-armed combatants avidly pouncing on their opponents. Meanwhile, in the river, all kinds of fish are depicted trying to swim away from the lethal blows of the contenders. On the bank, hesitant-looking wild ducks seem to watch the scene with interest.
Mastaba of Akhuthotep and Ptahhotep,
Old Kingdom,
Saqqara, Lower Egypt.

before completion, and the "King's Chamber." It is accessed by a gallery, 160 feet long and 30 feet high, which leads to a small room containing a monolithic sarcophagus whose lid has disappeared. The real reasons which led the architects to modify the arrangement of the interior chambers so many times remain unknown: royal decision, a fear of desecration, technical constraints? Nobody can say.

Near the south east face of the pyramid, a modern building contains one of the most spectacular discoveries made on the plateau of **Giza**: a remarkable boat made of Lebanese cedar, 20 feet wide and 150 feet long. It was discovered in 1954 by the Egyptian Antiquities Service during the clearance of an area south of the pyramid. Forty one limestone blocks, each weighing 18.8 tons, hid a long nave-shaped chamber in which the boat, divided into pieces, was carefully arranged. The reconstruction and restoration of some six hundred and fifty pieces totalling one thousand two hundred and twenty four pieces of wood required nearly fourteen years of work. Not far from there, the archaeologists discovered a second pit; it also contained a wooden boat which in all likelihood is identical to the first. It will be unearthed when the problems linked to the conservation of this object have been resolved.

Three satellite pyramids stand along the face of the royal pyramid: these are the queens' pyramids. According to **Herodotus**, the pyramid in the centre belonged to the daughter of **Khufu** who built it the following way: finding himself short of funds to finish the works of his royal tomb, the king would have placed his daughter in a house of debauchery so she could earn the necessary sum to finish his grandiose project. *"The girl obeys her father, but she too desires a monument in her name; for this reason, she requests each of her visitors to gift her with a stone. With these stones, I was explained, the three pyramids were built. These are pyramids which are at the centre of the group in front of the great pyramid and which measures a plethe and a half a side (150 feet)".* If the measuring is bona fide, one finds it most regrettable that the Greek did not care to elaborate a bit on his narrative. In any case, the building does not belong to a daughter of **Khufu** but to one of his half sisters.

Khafra, one of the sons of **Khufu** who also reigned in the 4th Dynasty, established his funeral complex to the south of his father's. It is the best preserved structure of the necropolis: besides the pyramid, the funeral temple, the causeway and, above all, the valley temple, also known as the "T-shaped" or the "granite temple", are all visible. The complex is entered by two gates, formerly guarded by sphinxes, giving onto a vestibule and then a large room in the form of an inverted T whose ceiling has

Khufu's Boat

Khufu's boat was found in 1954, when the area south of the great pyramid was being cleared by the Egyptian Antiquities Service. Too large to be stored in the chamber that was created for it, it had been dismantled and carefully put away in detached pieces. To reconstruct this puzzle of six hundred and fifty elements, totalling one thousand two hundred and twenty four pieces of wood, archaeologists and restorers worked for fourteen years. Today, the royal boat stands in a museum situated to the south east of the pyramid of Khufu: it measures 20 feet wide by 150 feet long.
Khufu's boat,
Old Kingdom,
Giza, Lower Egypt.

disappeared. Nevertheless, the supporting pillars have withstood the ravages of both time and plunderers: these are solid monolithic blocks of pink granite from faraway **Aswan**. Diorite, shale and alabaster statues, discovered by *Mariette* at the bottom of a pit, stood against the walls. The most beautiful one, considered amongst the master-pieces of all-times sculpture, is on display at the **Egyptian Museum of Cairo**. As for the pyramid, it is quite up to the standard of *Khufu*'s. Although slightly shorter, it seems to tower above the "Great Pyramid" on the **Giza** plateau for two reasons: not only is it built on a higher point of elevation, but it also has retained its beautiful limestone casing at the apex which gives it its height of 476 feet, close to the present height of *Khufu*.

If the pyramids of *Khufu* and *Khafra* rival each other in size and beauty, such is not case with *Menkaura* which, on the **Giza** plateau, seems like an abandoned little sister. Isolated from its context, it would certainly be spectacular; unfortunately it is overshadowed by the presence of its elders to the extent that it is hardly looked at, if not altogether ignored. However, it rises to 217 feet and sits on a base of 378 feet a side. In 1837, the archaeologist *Howard Vyse* discovered a basalt tub inside the burial chamber; anepigraphic, yet decorated, it contained a wooden coffin inscribed with the names of *Menkaura*. The following year, the two objects were sent to England to join the collection at the **British Museum**. However, the *Beatrice,* a vessel carrying the stone sarcophagus, sank off the Iberian coast and, despite numerous searches, it could never be retrieved.

The excavations, led by *Reisner* in the valley temple of *Menkaure*, yielded some superb shale triads showing the king with the goddess *Hathor* and the personifications of the nomes, Egypt's provinces. Four statues of this type were found; could they, perhaps, have been originally intended for each province? It is a possibility that can be considered.

East of the plateau, not far from the granite temple of *Khafra*, sits *Harmakhis,* "*Horus* on the Horizon." This enormous rock-cut sphinx measures 70 feet high and more than 245 feet long. Facing eastwards, it custodies the western regions where the sun and the deceased disappear. Traditionally, it is dated from the reign of *Khafra*, but certain Egyptologists think that it could be much older. Whatever the case, in the Old Kingdom, it plays the role of protector of the **Giza** necropolis. During the 18th Dynasty, it acquires certain characteristics of the Sun which identify it with the god *Ra-Atum-Khepri,* creator of **Heliopolis**. This is confirmed by a stele placed between the paws of an animal by *Thutmose IV*: "*Look at me and admire me, oh Thutmose; I am your father, Harmakhis-Khepri-Ra-Atum.*" In this story, where *Harmakhis* appears in the form of a young prince, he learns that the sphinx is completely covered with sand. The god therefore asks *Thutmose*, his "*protector*" and his "*guide*", to liberate the sphinx from the smothering sands; in exchange he shall give him "*the royalty of the earth at the head of men.*" No sooner said than done, the sphinx is rescued and *Thutmose* rises to the throne of Egypt.

The Lights of Cairo

"The Nile, which was looked then as a small sea; the mixture of desert sand and fresh vegetation; palm groves, sycamores, the domes, mosques and minarets of Cairo; the far-off pyramids of Saqqara, where the river seems to come out of its immense reservoirs; all of this formes a picture that has no equal on earth." *Thus speaks Chateaubriand as he watches the city and its surroundings from the ship bringing him to Cairo. The sentence admirably portrays the capital of Egypt: the Nile, the desert and the oasis at the heart of an extraordinary amalgam of cultures where pharaohs stand alongside sultans.*
Cairo,
Lower Egypt.

Cairo

The plateau of **Giza** marks the last step of the "Route of the Pyramids". Beyond stretches **Cairo**, one of the biggest megalopolis of the world. In the entire African continent, there is no city homing as many living beings as Cairo. Latest estimates show more than 13 million inhabitants; the city was initially conceived for 3 million.

The origins of **Cairo** date back to the seventh century: in 639, *'Amr ibn el-As*, lieutenant of the Caliph *'Omar,* seizes the **"Fortress of Babylon"** and founds the town of **Fostat. Babylon**, which lies on the right bank of the Nile opposite the southernmost point of the **island of Roda**, is the name given in the Roman era to a small area of **Heliopolis**, the city of the Sun god. At that time, this small village was enclosed by a surrounding wall fitted with two watchtowers and four gates: the presumed **"Fortress of Babylon"**. Later, a Coptic community settled there; **Babylon** became **Qasr es-Sham**, the "Fortress of the Sun". When the lieutenant *'Amr* seizes this city he regards it as a mere step conducive to the takeover of **Alexandria**, then the capital of Egypt. A legend has it that when the camp was being raised to march on **Alexandria**, *'Amr* refused to dismantle his tent because two doves had nested on it. At this site, he founds a city, **Fostat**, and then builds the first mosque in the country. Nowadays, the ruins of the city are still visible, to the east of **Qasr es-Sham**; there are excavations under way which have shed light on the original layout of roads and houses. As for the mosque, considered one of the most ancient Muslim buildings in the country and in the entire Islam, it is still standing but, rebuilt over and over again, nothing is there to be seen of the original edifice. The area known under the name of **Old Cairo**, or **Coptic Cairo**, corresponds to the old town of **Qasr es-Sham**, where churches and convents can be found dating back to the arrival of the Copts. However, most of these buildings have been either transformed or rebuilt: this is the case of **Saint-Serge**, **Saint-Barbara**, **Saint-George** (better known under the name of **Mari Girgis**), or **el-Mo'llaqa** (also called **Saint-Mary**). In the ancient town, the **Coptic Museum**, founded at the beginning of the twentieth century, retraces its history to the first Christians of Egypt and displays pieces coming from all of the Nile valley. The town grows bigger under the *Umayyads*, then it passes to the hands of the *Abbassids* who rename it **al-'Askar**. In 870, *Ahmad ibn-Tulun* severs his ties to the caliphate of **Baghdad** and founds an independent dynasty, the *Tulunids,* which would rule Egypt for thirty five years. He establishes the capital on the hill of **Yashkur**, north-east of the Abbassid city, and gives it the name of **Al-Qata'i**. From the Tulunid town, which must have been remarkable, only the mosque remains. Considered as one of the greatest masterpieces of Islamic art. It is still intact, looking exactly as *ibn-Tulun* originally conceived it. The purity of its lines, the sobriety of its stucco décor and the perfect harmony of its proportions are its main features. From afar, the building can be recognized by its spiralled minaret, built like that of Iraq's **Samarra** mosque. According to legend, *ibn-Tulun*, an upright, solemn man, called a council to deal with the affairs of the country. At one moment, he lets his attention wander, absent-mindedly playing with a piece of paper that he wraps around his finger. With an amused air, one of his associates says to him: *"We have caught you in the midst of playing"*. To which the Tulunid leader replies: *"Not at all; I was in the midst of conceiving a new form of minaret."*

In 969, the *Fatimids*, already masters of North Africa, decide to seize Egypt. To lead this conquest successfully, *Gawhar al-Siquilli*, the commander in chief of the army, levies one hundred thousand men. They cross **Giza**'s plateau, then the Nile, and installed themselves north-east of **al-Qata'i**, along the desert hills of **Moqattam**. It is said that at the moment when works began for the foundation of the city, the planet **Mars** was ascending. Linked to war, Mars is also known as "the Victorious", **al-Qahir**; hence the name for the new city: **al-Qahira**, "the Victorious", or **Cairo**, in its English transcription. The main axis of the city was a road that permitted one to go from **Bab Zuwayla**, on the south, to **Bab al-Futuh** or **Bab al-Nasr**, on the north. It still exists: it is the **Sharia Mu'izz li Din Allah**, one of the most fascinating streets of **Cairo**. One realises that it does not keep a straight line but it slightly changes its direction every hundred metres; it is said to have been purposely built that way so that a part of the street is always shaded in the summer. No other place in **Cairo** can match the historical significance of this area: along its pavements, teeming with perfume and spice sellers, numberless Islamic monuments follow one another: **madrasas**, mausoleums, mosques, **sabils** (small tanks), caravanserais…

The Minarets of the al-Azhar Mosque
The mosque stands in the heart of the Fatimide area, not far from the Moqattam hills, east of Cairo. In its present state, it covers an area of around two and a half acres; it is Cairo's biggest. The original structure was, over the course of time, annexed several buildings: universities, colleges and libraries. Today, al-Azhar is the most prestigious and remarkable institution in both Egypt and the whole Islamic world.
Al-Azhar mosque,
Fatimide era,
Cairo.

Not all monuments dates back to the Fatimid era. The quarter, known under the name of **Islamic Cairo**, was much embellished and beautified under the *Ayyubids*, the *Mamluks* and the *Ottomans*. However, **al-Azhar** mosque is still the area's nerve centre. Founded in 970 by the *Fatimids*. **Al-Azhar** has become a symbol of Arab culture. It is home to the most prestigious university in the Islamic world, where, besides Islamic studies and Arabic, other fields such as commerce, agriculture, medicine, law or educational science, are also taught.

Under *Saladin*, founder of the Ayyubide dynasty, the neuralgic centre of the city moves south: **Cairo** is endowed with a citadel, situated on the foothills of **Moqattam**, which commands a view of **al-Qahira** to the right, **Fostat** to the left, and **al-Qata'i** on the front. Today, the original fortress is hard to recognise. It was enlarged and transformed by certain Mamluk and Ottoman sultans, and, in the nineteenth century, by *Muhammad Ali*, whose "Alabaster Mosque" stands south of the enclosure. The citadel allows a dazzling view of **Cairo**. The Nile flows in the middle, out of which the **islands of Roda** and **Gezirah** emerge. The town, sprawling and immense, spreads on both sides, wedged between **Giza** to the west and the hills of **Moqattam** to the east. To the south, the Nile valley comes to an end; to the north, the Delta unfolds. From its ramparts, the name given to **Cairo** —or to all of Egypt, for in Arabic they are both known as **Misr**— takes on all of its meaning: **Misr** is none other than **Umm ed-Donya**, the "Mother of the World."

Here five thousand years of history coalesce, pharaohs, caliphs and sultans all cohabiting alongside modern Cairo. There is no district, road, or alley where this extraordinary mixture of civilizations does not show. The modern city, built during the construction of the **Suez Canal**, stretches over the west bank of the Nile, between **Islamic Cairo** to the west, **Old Cairo** to the south, and the district of **Bulaq** to the north. All major roads converge towards the heart of the city: the **Midan at-Tahrir**, or "Liberty Square". Surrounded by hotels, administrative buildings, and above all the **Egyptian Museum**, which possesses the most important collection of Pharaonic antiquities in the world, the square always has a friendly atmosphere: taxis, buses, shoeshiners, street vendors and parking attendants add their cries to those of tourists, pedestrians, horns, and kids who offer tea, coffee, refreshing drinks… Despite the unbelievable hustle and bustle, everyone seems insouciant.

The **el-Tahrir** street leads to **el-Gumhuriya** Square (Square of the Republic), where the imposing **palace of 'Abdin** is located. After having served as a royal residence, it now houses various government departments. Next to it spreads the Islamic quarter, which welcomes the visitor with the majestic **Museum of Islamic Art**. It displays the superb pieces retracing the history of Muslim Egypt, from the *Umayyads* to the *Ottomans*: ceramics, wood carvings, coloured glass, inlaid metals, copperware, ivory, manuscripts. The **Ahmad Maher Pasha** street, leaving from the museum square, leads directly to **Bab Zuwayla**, which marks the entrance to the Fatimid city. Behind the mosque of **al-Azhar,** extends the **Khan el-Khalili**, the most celebrated bazaar in **Cairo**. Its creation dates back to the reign of the sultan *al-Ashraf Khalil,* one of the first *Mamluks*. It has been enlarged and transformed over the centuries to become an enormous market, visited both by locals and foreigners. Today its original purpose has been somewhat blurred by the huge number of stores selling tourist-aimed ware: jewellery, "Pharaonic souvenirs", local crafts, inlaid copperware, carpets, leather goods, perfumes… However, no sooner has one stepped on any of the small alleys off the **khan**'s main axis that a picturesque world comes into view where craftsmen can be found in front of their stalls hammering copper or chiselling it, blowing glass or colouring it, sculpting stone or engraving it. The din from the hammering mixes with the cries of tea-selling, **narguile**-offering children, the beeping horns of motorbikes and carriages, the braying of donkeys, the cheeping of birds… As for the passers-by, they stroll, they stop, they look over the merchandise, they bargain, they leave, they come back, they bargain again, they end up buying or sometimes they leave again… Only the call to prayer, five times a day from the muezzin, momentarily interrupts this incessant activity.

To the north stretches the residential quarter of **Misr el-gedid**, **New Cairo**, also called **Heliopolis**. It stands on either side of a wide avenue that leads to the airport. Created in 1905, this district includes the most beautiful villas in **Cairo**, especially that of *Baron Empain*, built in the purest "Khmer style." From the airport the roads start that lead towards the **Sinai** or towards the Delta of the Nile. From here one can travel to **Suez**, **Ismailia** or to **Port-Said**, towns between the Mediterranean and the **Gulf of Suez**, but also to any other town in the east or west Delta.

The East Delta

The Delta, "The Other Egypt," shows certain particularities that give this region a totally different character to that of the Nile Valley. Up to **Cairo**, the Nile was surrounded by narrow, desert-enclosed strips of cultivated land, whose size varied, at times to the point of non-existence, depending on the places. Beyond, until the Mediterranean Sea, the Delta fans out to form a great plain criss-crossed with channels and irrigated by the river, here split into two main branches. The Nile forks at the town of **el-Qanatir al-Qahiriya**, some twelve miles north east of **Cairo**; the **Damietta** branch heads to the east and the **Rosetta** branch heads to the west. On either side of their banks, as far as the eye can see, the most generous farmlands of the country spread out: vegetable gardens, cotton fields, mangoes, orange and lemon orchards…

All of these lands are richly irrigated by a clever system of channels which, seen from the sky, form a veritable web of small rivulets. The region is overpopulated: it is said that 45% of the Egyptian population lives within the triangle formed by **Cairo**, **Alexandria** and **Port-Said**.

Certainly, the Delta is covered with towns, villages and small simple hamlets which ceaselessly extend and multiply. To link these towns, a very dense network of roads criss-crosses the region. This infrastructure provides a shocking contrast to that of Upper Egypt, served by a single main road running along either the east or west bank the river, depending on what the Arabic and Libyan ranges allow.

Generally, the Delta is divided into two distinct regions by an imaginary border that could be situated at the town of **Benha**. It is here that the **Cairo** road ends, ramifying into two branches: one running eastwards and ending at **Damietta**, the other heading westwards and leading to **Alexandria**. Thus the terms east Delta and west Delta refer to the areas east and west of **Benha**. For the hurried visitor, the Delta is rarely a necessary stop. **Tanis** and **Alexandria**, the two most important historic sites of the region, are the two places most commonly visited. However, the occupation of the Delta dates back to the most ancient eras, and old towns and villages, often lost in the marshes, or simply destroyed and abandoned, are a common sight.

The Temple of Amun at Tanis

Tanis, capital of the Pharaohs of the 21st and 22nd Dynasties, is the most important site in the east Delta. It spreads over the Tell San el-Hagar, an enormous ancient mound almost 2 miles long. To the north, a double wall encloses different structures: the temple of Amun, the royal tombs, the sacred lake. The harmful effect of salt on the remains, mainly blocks and statues, has forced the Franco-Egyptian mission to work on the site and undertake important restorations on a yearly basis. The tent on the left was raised for this purpose; it permits the complete isolation of the pieces during the course of their restoration and protects them from the storms which in this region of Egypt can be quite violent. In this particular case, a small but spectacular storm has just borne down upon the site.
Temple of Amun,
Third Intermediate Period,
Tanis, Lower Egypt.

Actually, the two main factors contributing to their disappearance were the climate and human occupation. Contrary to the rest of the country, the Delta is under the influence of the Mediterranean Sea which causes harsh winters —violent winds, frequent rain, low temperatures— and hot and wet summers, conditions clearly not considered optimal for the conservation of antiquities. Furthermore, the **sebakh** searchers and the lime-kiln workers have greatly accelerated the pace of natural deterioration: the former pillaged the soil, the latter seized the construction stones. This plundering also exists in other parts of Egypt so it is only logical to ask why such practices afflict the Delta more than they do any other region —simply because, for many centuries, the **fellahs** have used, to fertilize their land, the highly productive soil, enriched with mineral and organic debris, found in ancient sites: the **sebakh**. In the Delta, the amount of agricultural land under cultivation has created a growing need for fertilizer, thus the increase in the number of **sebakh** searchers. As for the builders, they take the stones from ancient edifices, reusing them as an easy and inexpensive building material.

Today, efforts are being made, both by the Egyptian Antiquities Service and some foreign institutions, to revaluate the sites in the Delta, but the lack of tourist infrastructure and the rather poor quality of the roads certainly do not encourage visitors to venture in this region. Moreover, a phenomenon of saturation must certainly be taken into account: it is undeniable that for visitors coming from **Aswan**, **Luxor** or the "Route of the Pyramids", the strenuous visit to the dilapidated sites of the Delta might seem a bit too daunting. This region is perhaps better suited for the enlightened amateur than for the passing tourist. However, Egypt can only be seen but through its antiquities. What originality may the Delta possess must be found in its atmosphere, its ambience, its colour, its particular charm… Its marshes, bathed with a subdued light and cloaked with a thin veil of transparent mist are home to flamingos, herons, pelicans, waders and ducks whose playful cackling and squawking merge with the sounds of the animals from a nearby farm. In the distance, the noise from a water pump resonates and mixes with the creaking of the **noria** wheel, while on the edge of a channel, women, accompanied by their children, talk and laugh and shout while washing their laundry or their dishes.

The **Damietta** branch of the river leads directly to the town of **Benha** where, on its banks, lie the vestiges of ancient **Athribis** —present-day **Tell Atrib**—, capital of the tenth nome of Lower Egypt. Some texts explain that the foundation of the site dates back to the Old Kingdom, maybe the 4th Dynasty; however, the archaeological excavations on the site have not succeeded in locating any structure previous to the reign of *Ahmose*, king of the 26th Dynasty. Amongst the ruins there remain the last traces of the Greco-Roman city; the site was literally gnawed away by **sebakh** searchers, who, in 1924, discovered a treasure from the Late Period.

Leaving **Benha**, the road coming from **Cairo** branches off and thus connects with **Damietta** in the north, **Tanis** to the east and **Alexandria** to the west. The first one skirts the right bank of the river, and after having passed **Mit Ghamr**, it crosses the Nile to reach **Abu Sir**, the ancient **Busiris**. It was one of the holy towns of *Osiris,* the god of the dead, in which, according to *Herodotus*, stood *"a very great temple of Isis"*. Unfortunately, no traces remain. A few miles away is **Samannud**, the ancient **Sebennytos**, where only a few time-ravaged blocks can be found. Nevertheless, the town is famous, at least by name, since it is intimately linked to the historian *Manetho*. It is unknown whether he was originally from **Sebennytos**, or arrived there later in the role of a priest. Whatever the case, it is the man that matters. He lived in the third century B.C. and is a contemporary of the first *Ptolemies*. His masterpiece, the *Aegyptiaca*, is of primordial importance for it retraces nearly three thousand years of history. It is a complete and detailed list of one hundred and ninety kings of Egypt, from *Narmer,* first Pharaoh of the 1st Dynasty, to *Ptolemy II*. They are classified into thirty dynasties, which in turn are grouped into empires, the auspicious, magnificent periods, interspersed by the intermediate, troubled periods. Unfortunately, the original of the *Aegyptiaca* disappeared and the work of *Manetho* is only known through fragments recorded by later documents, notably those left by *Flavius Josefus* or *Eusebius of Cæsarea*. **Sebennytos** is the original town of pharaohs from the 30th Dynasty, reputed for their immense devotion to the goddess *Isis*; accordingly, they had a temple erected to her, the **Iseum**, on present-day **Behbeit el-Hagar**: The temple collapsed, maybe as a result of an earthquake, but a walk around its ruins allows one to admire the superb reliefs that decorated the walls.

**Colossus
of Ramesses II**

In the temple of Amun in Tanis, numerous blocks or fragments of statues date back to the Ramesside era. This is explained by the fact that the foundations of the temple are entirely made of elements, mostly quartz and granite, taken from Pi-Ramesses, the capital of the Ramesside kings. These pieces, which used to lie scattered all over the place, have been reassembled and restored, cleaned of salt deposits, and placed on pedestals to keep them off the ground. This is the case with this beautiful fragment of a Ramesses colossus in quartzite which stands at the entrance of the temple of Amun.
Temple of Amun,
Third Intermediate Period,
Tanis, Lower Egypt.

The Nile pushes on to complete its journey: it arrives at **Damietta**, and later to **Ras el-Barr** where the river empties into the Mediterranean Sea. To the east of these two towns lies the largest lake of the Delta, some 1,100 square miles: **Lake Manzala**. A town by the same name stands on its southern shore that leads, by way of a tortuous road, to **San el-Hagar**, the ancient **Tanis**. It is one of the most important sites in the Delta. The town makes its debut during the 21st Dynasty. At the beginning of the Third Intermediate Period, the power is divided: Upper Egypt is governed, in **Thebes**, by the clergy of *Amun* while the Pharaohs rule Lower Egypt from **Tanis**. Here *Psusennes I* and his successors devote themselves to the construction of the temple dedicated to the Theban triad: *Amun, Mut* and *Khons*. The town of **Tanis** is rediscovered in the nineteenth century by the archaeologist *Flinders Petrie*; a connection was established between it and both **Avaris**, the Hyksos capital, and **Pi-Ramesses**, the capital of the Ramessid era, by virtue of numerous blocks coming from these two areas and found at **Tanis**. Truly, the interpretation of this site is difficult. As a matter of fact, nothing more than a few granite vestiges from the Hyksos or Ramesses periods remain on the spot: these are the foundations of the temple built by the kings of the 21st Dynasty, which had the necessary material taken from the sites of **Pi-Ramesses** and **Avaris**, situated some miles to the south. The temple itself, limestone-built, rested on the purloined granite foundations, but very little remains of the structure: it has been totally pillaged by the limeworkers. Therefore, what one finds in **Tanis** is a temple of the Third Intermediate Period of which nothing remains except its foundations, built of second-hand stones inscribed with the name of *Ramesses II*. Under these circumstances, the connection with **Pi-Ramesses** is evident. From the reign of *Psusennes I* there remains an enormous brick enclosure which surrounded the site of the great temple to *Amun*. The "Monumental Gate" and most of the structures of the temple date from the 22nd Dynasty, but today it is difficult to find traces of these buildings. In effect, the works of the kings of the 30th Dynasty and the *Ptolemies* have blurred the origins of the remains since all of them remodelled and modified the sites of existing buildings and added new cult places. However the city was not limited to this single structure. The **Tanis** French Mission for Excavations unearthed numerous structures (temples, necropoleis, a sacred lake, dwellings, enclosures, shafts) extended over an area of two square miles.

The most fantastic of these discoveries was the royal necropolis, found by *Pierre Montet* in 1939. It contains the tombs, sometimes undisturbed, of certain Pharaohs of the 21st and 22nd Dynasties. The tombs of *Psusennes*, that of his minister *Undebaunded* and that of *Amenemope*, all contained rich funeral ornaments.

The road that leads to **Cairo** skirts the sites of **Pi-Ramesses** and of **Avaris**, locally known as **Qantir** and **Tell el-Dab'a**. However, almost nothing remains of these two towns that once served as capitals, the former in the Ramesside period, the latter in the Hyksos era. Lastly, past **Zaqaziq**, one of the largest towns in the Delta, the remains of **Tell Basta**, the ancient **Bubatis**, can be seen. They belong to the "House of *Bastet*", the cat goddess.

Considered one of the sun's daughters, *Bastet* embodies the pacific facets of the dangerous goddesses. *Herodotus* writes: *"In this town there is a temple dedicated to the goddess Bastet which deserves to be mentioned: others may be more sumptuous and more grandiose, but none is more pleasing to the eye."* He describes a temple located at the centre of the town and surrounded by water from two channels, which makes the temple look like an island. About the interior he says: *"a forest of gigantic trees surrounds the vast temple in which sits the statue of the goddess."* On the site, the truth of this description is impossible to assess since the form, size and aspect of the temple are all unknown. All that remains is a jumble of stones.

The West Delta

Different choices are on offer to the visitor who wants to see **Alexandria**. He can take the "agricultural route", which is convenient but lacks real interest: it is the highway that links the largest towns of the West Delta. A much more rewarding option would be for him to leave this road at **Tanta**, then follow the **Rosetta** branch of the Nile until the Mediterranean Sea. This route allows one to stop in **Sa el-Hagar**, on the banks of the river. Today, the site is abandoned: only a few blocks and raw brick structures remain visible. It marks the location of the ancient town of **Sais** which played an important political role in the Third Intermediate Period, then during Late Period.

Lake Manzala
Located in the north east of the Delta, Lake Manzala is separated from the sea by a very narrow strip of land stretching from Port-Said to Ras el-Barr. To the south, the town of Matariyya boasts a small yet busy harbour. It takes in the fishermen of Manzaleh who provide much of the Delta with fish.
Lake Manzala,
Lower Egypt.

Past the ruins of **Tell el Fara'in**, comprising some remains of the ancient town of **Buto**, the Nile reaches **Rosetta**, a small town with a quaint old-fashioned charm. Until the nineteenth century, its harbour controlled most sea traffic; then *Muhammad Ali* embarks upon his grand projects to expand **Alexandria** and **Rosetta** falls into obscurity. Today, it gives the impression of having been deserted. But its name remains one of the most celebrated in the Nile valley since it is linked to the stele which permitted the French *Champollion* to unravel the mystery of the hieroglyphics: the **"Rosetta Stone"**. It was discovered by a French officer in 1799 during construction work on a fortress situated a few miles from the town. Beyond, the road continues and reaches the place where the Nile meets the Mediterranean Sea. The coast can be followed all the way to **Alexandria**.

In 332 B.C., *Alexander the Great* enters Egypt and defeats the Persians. Weary of the Persian domination, the Egyptians hail Alexander as a liberator. During his journey to **Siwa** to consult the oracle of *Amun*, who shall proclaim him "Master of the Universe" and son of the god, he passes before **Rhakotis** and decides to build there the city of **Alexandria**. The architect *Dinocrates of Rhodes* strives to make the most out of the area's natural features. In front of the city, the **island of Pharos** stands like a natural barrier. Dinocrates has the island connected to the mainland by means of a mole, the Heptastadium, thus creating two harbours: one to the west, still used to this day, the second to the east, nowadays converted into a promenade-fringed roadstead. On the outermost tip of the island, at the actual location of the fortress of **Qaytbay**, *Sostrate of Cnidus* builds a big lighthouse designed to serve as a guide to sailors: the seventh Wonder of the World. The tower, inaugurated around 283 B.C. under the reign of *Ptolemy II Philadelphus*, measured more than 350 feet in height and was composed of three stages. It collapsed in the fourteenth century. Some centuries later, underwater archaeologists working at the foot of the **Qaytbay** fortress find an enormous site consisting of two thousand blocks: fragments of statues, sphinxes, capitals, columns, construction blocks, obelisks. Is it the lighthouse? Probably. However, until a dedicatory inscription reading *"Sosastros of Cnidus, son of Dexiphanes, dedicated this monument to the saviour gods for the salvation of sailors"* is found, the discovery will not be ratified. Similarly, the Heptastadium no longer exists. The **island of Pharos** has again become almost an island and the mole has transformed into a long strip of earth on which the Arab town stands. The plan of the ancient city is well known: it is inspired by the Hellenistic model with a network of orthogonal roads forming a regular grid pattern. Of the religious quarter, located at the heart of the city, nothing remains but the *Pompey's* Pillar, some fragments of statues and the entrance to the catacombs. It is here where the **Serapeum** stood, dedicated to the god of the Alexandrian city and of the *Ptolemaic* dynasty: *Sarapis*. Close to the ruins of the temple, the catacombs of **Kom el-Shugafa** make up a remarkable collection of tombs from the first and second centuries; the chambers are decorated with scenes delightfully fusing Egyptian and Hellenistic styles.

The heart of the old city, the **Brucheion**, stands by the sea shore. However, only the Roman theatre of **Kom el-Dikka** and the baths have resisted the onslaughts of time. From the royal palaces nothing remains; the same applies for both the Library or the Museum. The idea of providing the city with these institutions came from *Demetrius of Phaleron*. He fancied a building that would receive all kinds of scholars: grammarians, philosophers, poets, geographers, doctors, physicians, astronomers. The tools at their disposal: seven hundred thousand volumes comprising the sum of all that had been written in the Greek world. Neglected by *Caesar* and looted in the fourth century, it was definitively destroyed by the fire that razed **Alexandria** in 642 A.D. As for the tomb of *Alexander*, which excites the most passionate controversies, its exact location has not yet been discovered, despite the numerous attempts: one hundred and thirty nine to be exact.

Today, **Alexandria** plays the role of Egypt's second capital. Yet nothing in the city is profoundly Egyptian: there are no Pharaonic antiquities, rare Greco-Roman ruins, a non-existent Islamic quarter, and a river, the Nile, which seems only too glad to bypass the city and keep a distance. What is this city doing in Egypt? Resolutely cosmopolitan, and open to the sea, it is not an African but a Mediterranean city. Its ancient name *ad Aegyptum*, "On the edge of Egypt", perfectly describes it. Perhaps its attraction lies in this difference. Here one rambles down streets evoking not pharaohs nor sultans, but khedives and kings; it is an immense pleasure. This **Alexandria** of the twentieth century, tinged with charm and melancholy, emerges with every step along its wide avenues, its buildings, its seafront, its shaded corniche...

THE NILE VALLEY

Sedeinga
18th Dynasty temple dedicated to Queen *Tiy*, spouse of *Amenhotep III*

Soleb
Temple of *Amenhotep III*

Tombos
Rock inscriptions from the New Kingdom

Kerma
Capital of the Nubian kingdom (**Kush**) from 2400 B.C. (Egyptian Old Kingdom) until 1500 B.C. (Egyptian New Kingdom) including a town and necropolis

Dongola el-Aguz
Vestiges from the Christian and Arab eras

el-Kurru
Necropolis including the pyramids of **Napata**'s first kings and of 25th Dynasty kings

Nuri
Necropolis including the tombs of most Nubian kings, from *Taharqo* (664 B.C.) to 300 B.C.

Napata
Capital of the Nubian kingdom from the beginning of the ninth century B.C. (slightly before the 25th Dynasty) until the fourth century B.C.; temples dedicated to the Theban triad, built at the foot of **Gebel Barkal**

Meroe
Capital of the Nubian kingdom between the fourth century B.C. and the fourth A.D.; temples and pyramids from the Meroitic kingdom

Naga and Mussarawat
Sacred cities from the Meroitic era with structures dedicated to the lion god *Apedemak* and to the Egyptian god *Amun*

THE SOURCES OF THE NILE

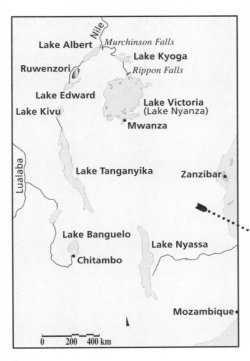

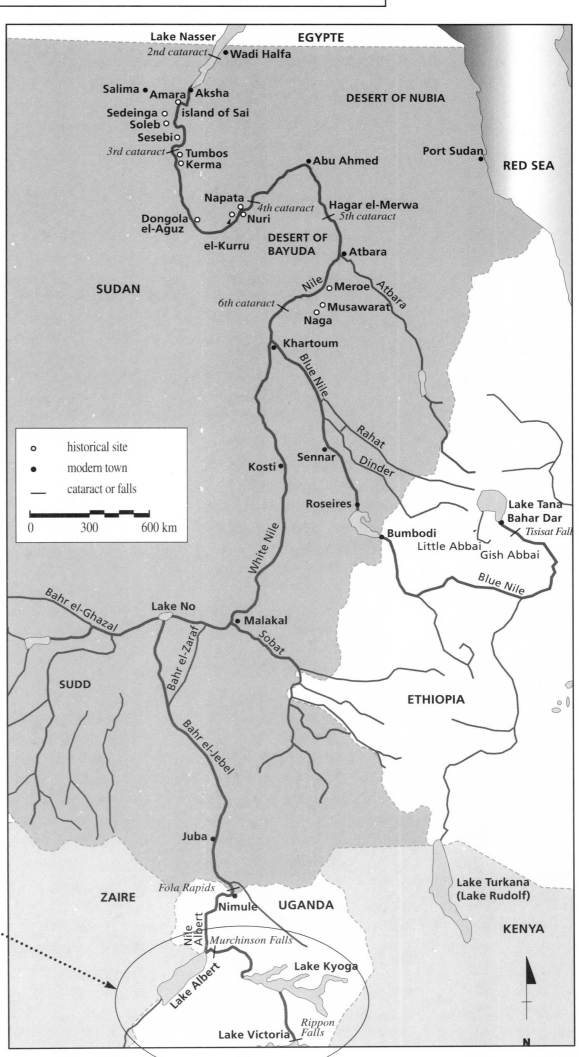

UPPER EGYPT

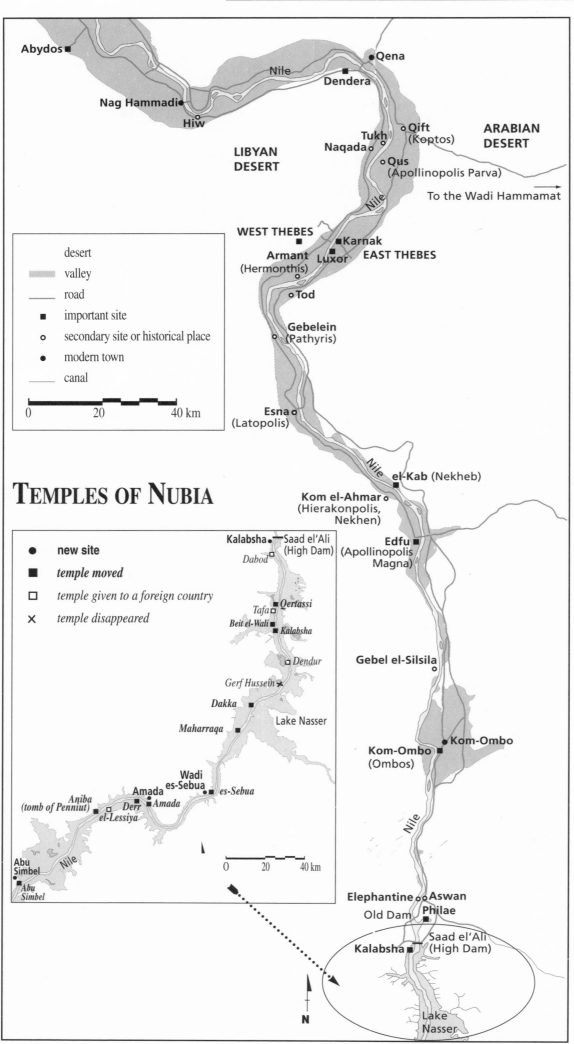

TEMPLES OF NUBIA

Legend (main map):
- desert
- valley
- road
- ■ important site
- ○ secondary site or historical place
- ● modern town
- canal

0   20   40 km

Legend (Temples of Nubia):
- ● new site
- ■ *temple moved*
- □ *temple given to a foreign country*
- × *temple disappeared*

0   20   40 km

N

Map labels (main map):
Abydos, Nag Hammadi, Hiw, Nile, Qena, Dendera, LIBYAN DESERT, Tukh, Naqada, Qift (Koptos), ARABIAN DESERT, Qus (Apollinopolis Parva), To the Wadi Hammamat, WEST THEBES, Karnak, EAST THEBES, Armant (Hermonthis), Luxor, Tod, Gebelein (Pathyris), Esna (Latopolis), Nile, el-Kab (Nekheb), Kom el-Ahmar (Hierakonpolis, Nekhen), Edfu (Apollinopolis Magna), Gebel el-Silsila, Kom-Ombo (Ombos), Nile, Elephantine, Aswan, Old Dam, Philae, Kalabsha, Saad el'Ali (High Dam), Lake Nasser

Map labels (Temples of Nubia):
Kalabsha, Saad el'Ali (High Dam), Dabod, Tafa, Qertassi, Beit el-Wali, Kalabsha, Dendur, Gerf Hussein, Dakka, Maharraqa, Lake Nasser, Amada, Wadi es-Sebua, es-Sebua, Aniba (tomb of Penniut), Amada, Derr, el-Lessiya, Abu Simbel, Abu Simbel, Nile

Hiw
Two Greco-Roman temples and necropolis from different periods

Dendera
Ptolemaic temple to the goddess *Hathor*

Qift (former Koptos)
City of the god *Min*, patron of eastern desert routes

Nagada and Tukh
Tombs from the pre-dynastyc period and from the two first dynasties, hence the term "nagadian", denoting certain ancient cultures

Qus (former Apollinopolis Parva)
Remains from a Greek temple dedicated to *Haroeris* and the frog goddess *Heqet*

West Thebes
Necropolis and funerary temples of kings and officials from the New Kingdom (**Valley of the Kings, Colossi of Memnon, Deir el-Bahri, Ramesseum, Medinet Habu**…)

East Thebes
Temples of **Luxor** and **Karnak** devoted to the Theban triad: *Amun, Mut* and *Khons*

Armant and Tod
Middle Kingdom temples devoted to *Montu*, warrior god of the Empire

Gebelein
Tombs from the First Intermediate Period

Esna
Greco-Roman temple dedicated to *Khnum*, seen in this city as a god of creation

el-Kab (former Nekheb)
Town and temple of the vulture goddess *Nekhbet*, patroness of Upper Egypt

Kom el Ahmar (former Hierakonpolis)
City of *Horus of Nekhen;* necropolis, temples and structures of the pre-dynastic period

Edfu (former Apollinopolis Magna)
City of *Horus Behedety; Horus* temple

Gebel el-Silsila
Horemheb speos; quarries exploited from the 18th Dynasty until the end of the Greco-Roman era

Kom Ombo (former Ombos)
Greco-roman temple dedicated to crocodile god *Sobek* and falcon god *Haroeris*

Elephantine
Temple dedicated to *Khnum, Satis* and *Anukis*, custodian divinities of the sources of the Nile

Aswan
Granite quarries; incomplete obelisk

Philae
Greco-Roman *Isis* temple

Kalabsha
Group of Unesco-reconstructed sanctuaries (**Kalabsha, Qertassi** and **Beit el-Wali**)

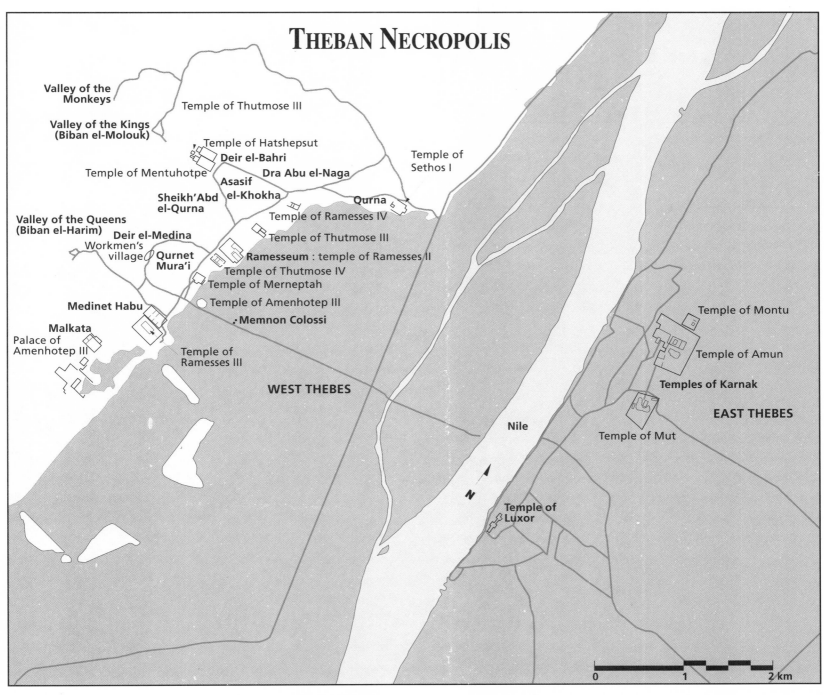

THEBAN NECROPOLIS

Valley of the Monkeys

Temple of Thutmose III

Valley of the Kings (Biban el-Molouk)

Temple of Hatshepsut

Deir el-Bahri

Temple of Mentuhotpe

Dra Abu el-Naga

Asasif el-Khokha

Temple of Sethos I

Sheikh'Abd el-Qurna

Qurna

Temple of Ramesses IV

Valley of the Queens (Biban el-Harim)

Deir el-Medina

Temple of Thutmose III

Workmen's village

Qurnet Mura'i

Ramesseum : temple of Ramesses II

Temple of Thutmose IV

Temple of Merneptah

Medinet Habu

Temple of Amenhotep III

Malkata

Memnon Colossi

Palace of Amenhotep III

Temple of Ramesses III

Temple of Montu

Temple of Amun

Temples of Karnak

WEST THEBES

EAST THEBES

Temple of Mut

Nile

Temple of Luxor

N

0   1   2 km

el-Badari

Ancient sepulchres; the term "badarian" denotes certain Upper Egyptian Neolithic and Eneolitic cultures

Qaw el-Kebir

Civil tombs from the 12th Dynasty

Akhmim

Chapel of *Thutmose III* and Greco-Roman temples devoted to *Min*

Sohag

The White and Red Convents

Wannina (former **Athribis**)

Ptolemaic temples and tombs

Nag el-Deir

Remains from the necropolis of **This**

Girga (former **This**)

Birthplace of the sovereigns from the two first dynasties, hence the term "Thinite kings" used to denote them

Beit Khallaf

3rd Dynasty tombs

Abydos

First holy city in Egypt dedicated to *Osiris;*
Osireion, necropolis from different eras and temples of *Sethos I* and *Ramesses II*

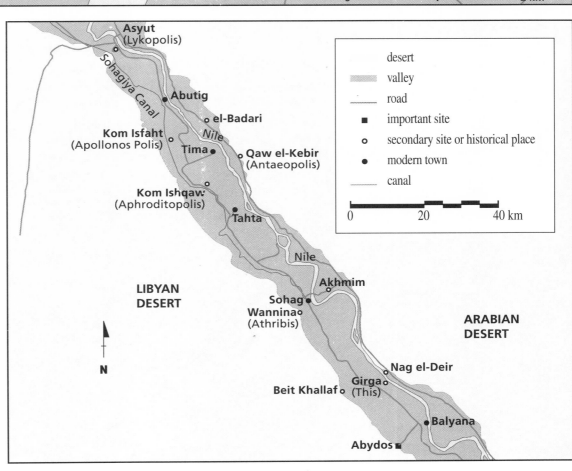

Asyut (Lykopolis)

Sohagiya Canal

Abutig

el-Badari

Kom Isfaht (Apollonos Polis)

Nile

Tima

Qaw el-Kebir (Antaeopolis)

Kom Ishqaw (Aphroditopolis)

Tahta

Nile

Akhmim

LIBYAN DESERT

Sohag

Wannina (Athribis)

ARABIAN DESERT

N

Nag el-Deir

Girga (This)

Beit Khallaf

Balyana

Abydos

desert

valley

road

■ important site

○ secondary site or historical place

● modern town

canal

0   20   40 km

MIDDLE EGYPT

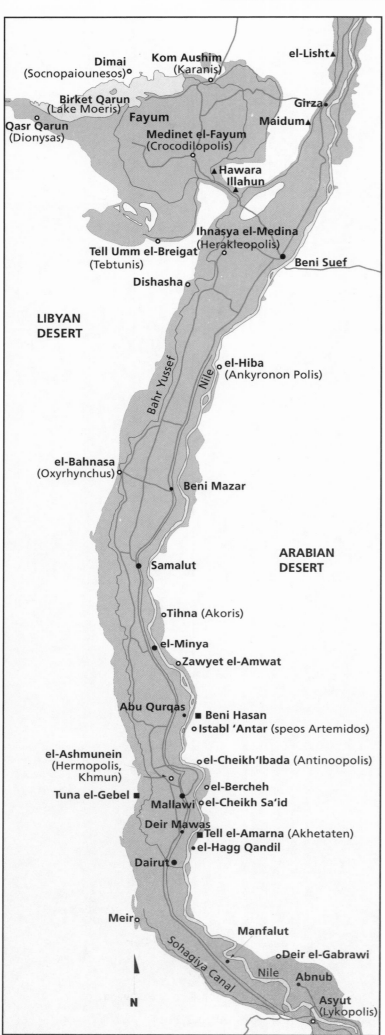

LIBYAN DESERT

ARABIAN DESERT

el-Lisht
12th Dynasty necropolis; pyramids of *Senusret I* and *Amenemhet I*

Maidum
Pyramid of *Huni/Sneferu*; necropolis from the beginning of the 4th Dynasty

Fayum region
Various sites from the Greco-Roman era, most of them dedicated to the crocodile god *Sobek*

Hawara
Pyramid of *Amenemhet III*

Illahun
Pyramid of *Senusret II*; sepulchres and **mastabas** from different periods

Ihnasya el-Medina (former **Herakleopolis**)
Tombs from the First Intermediate Period; 12th Dynasty temple dedicated to the god *Herishef*

Dishasha
Sepulchres from the end of the Old Kingdom

el-Hiba (former **Ankyronon Polis**)
Temple dating back to the reign of *Sheshonq I*

Tihna (former **Akoris**)
Cave tombs from the Old Kingdom; Greco-Roman necropolis and sanctuaries

Zawiet el-Amwat
Cave tombs belonging to the Old Kingdom; remains from a step pyramid (3rd Dynasty?)

Beni Hasan
Cave tombs belonging to nomarchs from the 11th and 12th Dynasties

Istabl 'Antar (speos **Artemidos**)
Rock-cut temple built by *Hatshepsut* and dedicated to the lioness goddess *Pakhet*

el-Cheikh'Ibada (former **Antinoopolis**)
City founded by *Hadrian* in memory of his loved *Antinoos*, drowned in that place

el-Ashmunein (former **Hermopolis**)
City of the ibis god *Thoth;* remains from 12th Dynasty edifices; pylon from the Ramessid era; Christian basilica

Tuna el-Gebel
Akhetaten's Boundary Stelae; sacred baboon and ibis catacombs; necropolis from the first centuries A.D.; tomb of *Petosiris*

el-Bersha
Cave tombs of 12th Dynasty nomarchs

el-Cheikh Sa'id
Tombs of 6th Dynasty nomarchs

Tell el-Amarna
Capital of *Amenhotep IV-Akhenaten*

Meir
Civil tombs from the 6th and 12th Dynasties

Asyut (former **Lykopolis**)
Tombs from the First Intermediate Period and the Middle Kingdom

desert
valley
road
■ important site
○ secondary site or historical place
▲ site with pyramid(s)
● modern town
canal

0   20   40 km

Dahshur, Saqqara, Abusir, Zawiet el-Aryan, Giza and **Abu Rawash**
Necropolis on the "Route of the Pyramids"

Heliopolis
City of *Ra*, the Sun god; tombs and structures from different periods; obelisk of *Senusret I*

LOWER EGYPT

MEDITERRANEAN SEA

Baltim
Ras el-Barr
Lake Burullus
Damietta
Rosetta
Port-Said
Lake Menzala
qir
ku
Sidi Sâlim
el-Matariya
fr el-Dauwâr
Tell el-Fara'in (Buto)
Shirbin
Disuq
el-Menzala
Kafr el-Sheikh
Behbeit el-Hagar
(Iseum)
Dikirnis
Kom el-Kanater
Sakha (Xois)
el-Mansura
Damanhur
(Hermopolis
Parva)
San el-Hagar
(Tanis)
Tell Dafana
(Daphnae)
Sa el-Hagar
(Sais)
el-Mahalla el-Kubra
Tell el-Rub'a (Mendes)
Tell el-Timai (Thmuis)
Naukratis
Abu Sir
(Bousiris)
Samannud
(Sebennytos)
el-Simbellawein
el-Qantara
Tanta
Qantir (Pi-Ramsès)
Tell el-Dab'a (Avaris)
Abu Kebir
Zifta
Mit Ghamr
Suez Canal
Faqûs
Tell Basta
(Bubastis)
Wadi Tumilat
Ismailia
Shibin el-Kom
Zagazig
Wadi Natrun
Minuf
Damietta Branch
Tell el-Maskhuta
(Pithom ?)
Tell Atrib (Athribis)
Benha
Bilbeis
Great
Bitter
Lake
Rosetta Branch
Shibin
el-Qanatir
Tell el-Yahudiya
(Leontopolis)
el-Qanatir
al-Qahiriya
Nile
ARABIAN DESERT
Heliopolis
To Suez
CAIRO
Abu Rawach
Giza
Zawiet el-Aryan
Mit Rahina
(Memphis)
Abusir
Saqqara
LIBYAN DESERT
Dahshur
N
Nile
el-Lisht

Tell el-Yahudiya
Middle Kingdom (?) complex with a palace of *Ramesses II* (?); ruins of the Jewish town and *Onia*'s temple

Tell Atrib (former **Athribis**)
Greco-Roman necropolis and temples

Tell Basta (former **Bubastis**)
City of the goddess *Bastet;* sanctuaries and necropolis of sacred animals (cats)

Tell el-Rub'a and **Tell el-Timai**
Old Kingdom **mastabas;** Greco-Roman structures; necropolis of sacred rams; temple of *Amasis*

Qantir et **Tell el-Dab'a**
Respectively identified as the ruins of the ancient towns of **Pi-Ramesses**, the Ramessid capital (**Qantir**), and **Avaris**, the Hyksos capital (**Tell el-Dab'a**)

San el-Hagar (former **Tanis**)
Capital of the Lower Egyptian kings from the 21th and 22th Dynasties; complex including the temple of *Amun*, royal tombs and the sacred lake

Abusir (former **Taposiris**)
Ptolemaic temple; necropolis of sacred animals; Roman tower (maybe a replica of **Alexandria**'s pharos)

Alexandria
Capital of the Ptolemaic dynasty

Tell el-Fara'in (former **Buto**)
City of the cobra goddess *Wadjit*, patroness of Lower Egypt

Behbeit el-Hagar (the **Iseum**)
Greco-Roman *Isis* temple

Sa el-Hagar (former **Sais**)
Remains from the temple of *Neith*

THE "ROUTE OF THE PYRAMIDS"

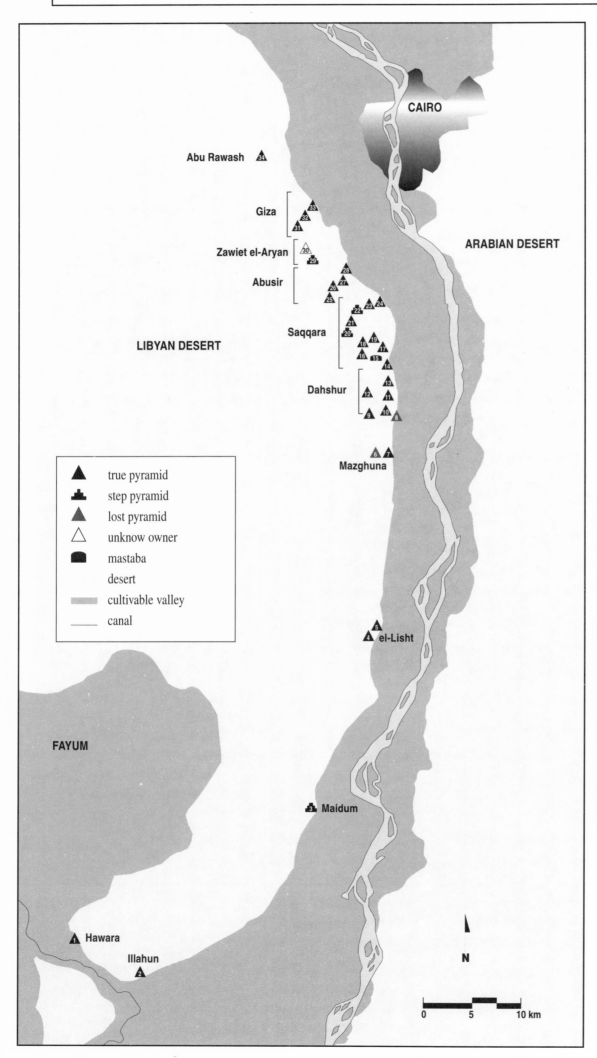

CAIRO

Abu Rawash

Giza

Zawiet el-Aryan

Abusir

ARABIAN DESERT

Saqqara

LIBYAN DESERT

Dahshur

Mazghuna

▲ true pyramid
🏛 step pyramid
▲ lost pyramid
△ unknow owner
⬛ mastaba
desert
▨ cultivable valley
— canal

el-Lisht

FAYUM

Maidum

Hawara

Illahun

N

0   5   10 km

HAWARA

1   *Amenemhet III* (12th Dynasty)

ILLAHUN

2   *Senusret II* (12th Dynasty)

MAIDUM

3   *Huni/Sneferu* (3rd/4th Dynasties)

EL-LISHT

4   *Senusret I* (12th Dynasty)
5   *Amenemhet I* (12th Dynasty)

MAZGHUNA

6   *Amenemhet IV?* (12th Dynasty)
7   *Sebekneferura?* (12th Dynasty)

DAHSHUR

8   *Menkauhor* (5th Dynasty)
9   *Sneferu* (4th Dynasty)
10   *Amenemhet III* (12th Dynasty)
11   *Amenemhet II* (12th Dynasty)
12   *Sneferu* (IVth Dynasty)
13   *Senusret III* (12th Dynasty)

SAQQARA

14   *Khendjer* (13th Dynasty)
15   *Shepseskaf* (4th Dynasty)
16   *Pepy II* (6th Dynasty)
17   *Djedkara-Izesi* (5th Dynasty)
18   *Merenra* (6th Dynasty)
19   *Pepy I* (6th Dynasty)
20   *Sekhemkhet* (3rd Dynasty)
21   *Unas* (5th Dynasty)
22   *Djoser* (3rd Dynasty)
23   *Userkaf* (5th Dynasty)
24   *Teti* (5th Dynasty)

ABUSIR

25   *Raneferef* (5th Dynasty)
26   *Neferirkara-Kakai* (5th Dynasty)
27   *Nyuserra-Ini* (5th Dynasty)
28   *Sahura* (5th Dynasty)

ZAWIET EL-ARYAN

29   *Khaba* (3rd Dynasty)
30   owner unknown

GIZA

31   *Menkaura* (4th Dynasty)
32   *Khafra* (4th Dynasty)
33   *Khufu* (4th Dynasty)

ABU RAWASH

34   *Djedefra* (4th Dynasty)

PHARAOH	N°	TYPE	LOCATION	MATERIAL	BASE / HEIGH	REMARKS
3rd Dynasty						
Djoser	22	step pyramid	**North Saqqara**	stone	121 x 109 / 60	
Sekhemkhet	20	step pyramid	**North Saqqara**	stone	119 x 119	uncompleted
Khaba	29	step pyramid	**Zawiet el-Aryan**	stone	79 x 79	uncompleted
Huni	3	step pyramid	**Maidum**	stone	144 x 144 / 93,5	collapsed
4yh Dynasty						
Sneferu	9	rhomboidal pyramyd	**Dahshur**	stone	183,5 x 183,5 / 105	
Sneferu	12	true pyramid	**Dahshur**	stone	220 x 220 / 104	
Khufu	33	true pyramid	**Giza**	stone	230 x 230 / 146	
Djedefra	34	true pyramid	**Abu Rawach**	stone	105 x 105	uncompleted
Khafra	32	true pyramid	**Giza**	stone	215 x 215 / 143,5	
Menkaura	31	true pyramid	**Giza**	stone	105 x 105 / 65,5	
Shepsekaf	15	mastaba	**South Saqqara**	stone	100 x 74	
5th Dynasty						
Userkaf	23	true pyramid	**North Saqqara**	stone	73,5 x 73,5 / 49	
Sahura	28	true pyramid	**Abusir**	stone	78,5 x 78,5 / 47	
Neferirkara-Kakai	26	true pyramid	**Abusir**	stone	108 x 108 / 70	
Shepsaskara	-					not found
Raneferef	25	true pyramid	**Abusir**	stone	65 x 65	
Nyuserra-Ini	27	true pyramid	**Abusir**	stone	81 x 81 / 51,5	
Menkauhor	8	true pyramid	**Dahshsur**	stone		not found
Djedkara-Izezi	17	true pyramid	**South Saqqara**	stone	78,5 x 78,5 / 52,5	
Unas	21	true pyramid	**North Saqqara**	stone	57,5 x 57,5 / 43	"Pyramid texts"
6th Dynasty						
Teti	24	true pyramid	**North Saqqara**	stone	78,5 x 78,5 / 52,5	"Pyramid texts"
Pepy I	19	true pyramid	**South Saqqara**	stone	78,5 x 78,5 / 52,5	"Pyramid texts"
Merenra	18	true pyramid	**South Saqqara**	stone	78,5 x 78,5 / 52,5	"Pyramid texts"
Pepy II	16	true pyramid	**South Saqqara**	stone	78,5 x 78,5 / 52,5	"Pyramid texts"
12th Dynasty						
Amenemhet I	5	true pyramid	**el-Lisht**	stone	78,5 x 78,5 / 55	
Senusret I	4	true pyramid	**el-Lisht**	stone	105 x 105 / 61	
Amenemhet II	11	true pyramid	**Dahshsur**	stone	50 x 50 ?	destroyed
Senusret II	2	true pyramid	**Illahun**	mud-brick	105 x 105 / 48	
Senusret III	13	true pyramid	**Dahshur**	mud-brick	105 x 105 / 78,5	
Amenemhet III	1	true pyramid	**Hawara**	mud-brick	103 x 103 / 58	
Amenemhet III	10	true pyramid	**Dahshsur**	mud-brick	105 x 105 / 81,5	cenotaph
Amenemhet IV?	6	true pyramid	**Mazghuna**	stone		not found
Sebekneferura?	7	true pyramid	**Mazghuna**	mud-brick	52,5 x 52,5	destroyed
13th Dynasty						
Khendjer	14	true pyramid	**South Saqqara**	brick	52,5 x 52,5 / 37 ?	lost

NB - The dimensions (base and height) are given in metres. They correspond to present-day, not original, dimensions.

TROUGH THE AGES

THE THINITE ERA
3150 to 2686 B.C.
Egypt is unified under the authority of a single king. The religion, administration, writing and art attain their almost definitive forms. Foreign countries are beginning to be dominated.

1st Dynasty	Narmer
	Aha
	Djer
	Djet
	Den
	Andjib
	Semerkhet
	Qa'a
2nd Dynasty	Hetepsekhemwy
	Raneb
	Nynetjer
	Peribsen
	Khasekhemwy

THE OLD KINGDOM
2686 to 2181 B.C.
This is the era of classical Egypt. The sovereigns establish their capital at **Memphis**. The country reaches a degree of exceptional refinement. Stone architecture appears and the Pharaohs build sepulchres in the shape of pyramids at **Dahshur**, **Giza** or **Saqqarah**. The 6th Dynasty shows a decline in Pharoanic authority, whilst the provincial governors, the **nomes**, continue growing. Their position, becomes hereditary, allowing the creation of veritable dynasties sometimes stronger than the king. The **nomes** quickly take their independence and the country is threatened by invaders. The monarchy doesn't succeed in addressing the situation and Egypt plunges into a period of troubles.

3rd Dynasty	Djoser
	Sekhemkhet
	Khaba
	Huni
4th Dynasty	Sneferu
	Khufu
	Djedefra

	Khafra
	Menkaura
	Shepseskaf
5th Dynasty	Userkaf
	Sahura
	Neferirkara-Kakai
	Shepseskara
	Raneferef
	Nyuserra
	Menkauhor
	Djedkara-Izezi
	Unas
6th Dynasty	Teti
	Pepy I
	Merenra
	Pepy II

THE FIRST INTERMEDIATE PERIOD
2181 to 2060 B.C.
It is the most complete anarchy: the petty kings take power, the nobles are dispossessed, the land is not cultivated, the flood is not exploited and famine takes hold of Egypt. Unfortunately, documents concerning this troubled period are rare, and, when they do exist, they are always from periods after the events described; for this reason very little is known about this era in Egyptian history.

7th Dynasty *(completely unknown)*

8th Dynasty *(originating from Memphis)*
	Wadjkara
	Kakara Ibi

9th/10th Dynasties *(originating from Herakleopolis)*
	Khety I
	Merykara
	Neferkara
	Khety II

11th Dynasty *(originating from Thebes and parallel to the end of the 10th Dynasty)*
	Mentuhotpe I
	Intef I
	Intef II
	Intef III

THE MIDDLE KINGDOM
2060 to 1782 B.C.
These are the princes of **Thebes** who were to unify Egypt under one single authority. In the fifteenth year of his reign *Mentuhotpe I* becomes king of Upper and Lower Egypt. This new era of prosperity, governed by the *Senusret* and the *Amenemhet*, is characterized by numerous political, administrative and religious reforms. The economic progress leads to the exploitation of new lands: **Fayum** and **Sinai**, the western desert, the eastern desert and Nubia. However, the 12th Dynasty ends in famine, disorder, internal disputes and foreign invasion for reasons that remain very obscure.

11th Dynasty	Mentuhotpe II
	Mentuhotpe III
	Mentuhotpe IV
12th Dynasty	Amenemhet I
	Senusret I
	Amenemhet II
	Senusret II
	Senusret III
	Amenemhet III
	Amenemhet IV
	Sebekneferura

THE SECOND INTERMEDIATE PERIOD
1782 to 1570 B.C.
It seems clear that the arrival of the **Hyksos** in Egypt, the "Foreigner Princes", is the origin of the destabilisation of the country. Reigning sometimes over Lower Egypt and other times over the whole country, they make their capital at **Avaris,** in the north east of the Delta, but, from the beginning of the 17th Dynasty, the princes of **Thebes** take the royal title and embark on a war to liberate the country from the invaders.

13th Dynasty *(Egyptian dynasty during which the kings, of Egyptian origin, seem to once again reign over the two kingdoms of Egypt; the capital is established at Iti-Tawi, in Fayum region)*
	Wegaf
	Ameny Intef IV
	Hor
	Sebekhotpe II

Khendjer
Nehesy
Sebekhotpe III
Neferhotpe I
Sebekhotpe IV
Aya
Neferhotpe II

14th Dynasty (*parallel to the end of the 13th Dynasty, it ends in a mysterious manner; the 14th Dynasty only reigns over the east Delta*)
Nehesy

15th/16th Dynasties (*dynasties which the kings Hyksos, originating from Asia, took power in Egypt and found their capital at Avaris*)
Sharek
Yakub-Har
Khyan
Apepi I
Apepi II
Anather
Yakobaam

17th Dynasty (*originally from Thebes, this dynasty attempts to re-conquer the country by fighting the Hyksos*)
Sebekemsaf II
Intef VII
Taa I
Taa II
Kamose

THE NEW KINGDOM
1570 to 1070 B.C.

This Empire marks a new era of prosperity and refinement: a revival of the royal strength, great territorial expansion, and an increasing flow of wealth towards Egypt. The kings found their capital at **Thebes**, the "City of Hundred Doors", which becomes a symbol of wealth and luxury. It is the sumptuous era of the Pharaohs *Thutmose* and *Amenhotep,* of the queen *Hatshepsut,* the heretic couple *Akhenaten* and *Nefertiti,* of the young *Tutankhamun,* of the sovereigns *Sethos* and *Ramesses.* However, the omnipresence of the clergy in the affairs of State lead to a degradation of the power of the Pharaohs. The Empire, weakened by intrigues, usurpations of power and internal conflict, can no longer resist invaders who are more and more on its very borders. Egypt will not recover from this slow decline.

18th Dynasty
Ahmose
Amenhotep I
Thutmose I
Thutmose II
Hatshepsut
Thutmose III
Amenhotep II
Thutmose IV
Amenhotep III
Amenhotep IV–Akhenaten
Smenkhkara
Tutankhamun
Ay
Horemheb

19th Dynasty
Ramesses I
Sethos I
Ramesses II
Merneptah
Amenmessu
Sethos II
Siptah
Tausret

21th Dynasty
Sethnakhte
Ramesses III
Ramesses III/Ramesses XI

THE THIRD INTERMEDIATE PERIOD
1070 to 656 B.C.

Egypt goes into a slow but irreversible decline. Exterior threats combine with internal difficulties. For the 21st and 22nd Dynasties, the Theban clergy reigns in the south, while the Pharaohs establish themselves in **Tanis** and rule the north. The 25th Dynasty is Ethiopian: *Piy*, king of **Napata**, takes power and little by little subjugates the south of the country. *Shabaqo*, his successor, establishes his capital in **Thebes** from where he conquers the Delta.

21st Dynasty (*presence of two royal houses: the priest kings reigning over Upper Egypt from Thebes; Smendes proclaims himself king at the death of Ramesses XI reigning over Lower Egypt from Tanis*)

Tanis	Thebes
Smendes I	Herihor
Amenemnisu	Piankh
Psusennes I	Pinudjem I
Amenemope	Masaharta
Osorkon the Elder	Menkheperre'
Siamun	Smendes II
Psusennes II	Pinudjem II

22nd Dynasty (*Libyan dynasty, originating from Bubastis, reigning in Tanis*)
Sheshonq I
Osorkon I
Sheshonq II
Takelot I
OsorkonII
Takelot II
Sheshonq III
Pimay
Sheshonq V
Osorkon IV
Harsiesis

23rd Dynasty (*a dynasty parallel to the end of the 22nd Dynasty which reigned in the Delta and Lower Egypt while the 23rd ruled, from Leontopolis, over Middle Egypt*)
Pedubastis I
Sheshonq IV
Osorkon III
Takelot III
Rudamon
Iuput

24th Dynasty (*the first dynasty of Sais*)
Tefnakht
Bocchoris

XXV dynasty (*a dynasty of Nubian origin: the kings of Napata take power and rule over Nubia and Egypt*)
Piy
Shabaqo
Shabitqo
Taharqo
Tanutamani

THE LOWER ERA
656 to 332 B.C.

This era marks the end of the independence of Pharaonic Egypt. It is characterised by a series of wars, invasions, intrigues and foreign dynasties. Only the 30th Dynasty, founded by the king *Nectanebo I*, succeeds in reviving the brilliance of the Pharaonic past.
Nectanebo II repels a Persian attack in 351 B.C. but, ten years later, *Artaxerxes III,* subjugates the country for the second time: he invades Egypt, driving **Nectanebo II** from power and founds the 31st Dynasty, often called the "Second Persian Domination".

26th Dynasty *(the second dynasty of Sais)*

        Psammetique I

        Nechao

        Psammetique II

        Apries

        Ahmose

        Psammetique III

27th Dynasty *(the First Persian Domination)*

        Cambyse

        Darius I

        Xerxes

        Artaxerxes I

        Darius II

        Artaxerxes II

28th Dynasty   Amyrtaios

29th Dynasty   Nepherites I

        Hakor

30th Dynasty   Nectanebo I

        Teos

        Nectanebo II

31st Dynasty *(Second Persian Domination)*

        Artaxerxes

        Arses

        Darius III Codoman

PTOLEMAIC EGYPT
332 to 30 B.C.

In 332 B.C. *Alexander the Great* enters Egypt and drives out the Persians. He founds the city of **Alexandria** and entrusts the government of Egypt to a satrap. Upon his death in 323 B.C. Egypt falls to one of his lieutenants, *Ptolemy*: he takes on the royal title in 305 B.C. and founds the Ptolemaic dynasty. Fourteen *Ptolemies* succeed to the throne of Egypt. The dynasty ends with *Cleopatra:* in 31 B.C., the battle of **Actium**, lost by *Antony*, is followed by the invasion of Egypt by the Legions of *Octavius.* After the suicide of *Antony*, *Cleopatra* delivers **Alexandria** to the new conqueror whom she attempts to seduce in order to save Egypt; in vain, she in turn takes her own life. In this way, Egypt becomes a province of the Roman Empire.

332 to 305 B.C.   Alexander the Great

        Philip Arrhidaeus

        Alexander IV

305 to 30 B.C.   Ptolemy I Soter I

        Ptolemy II Philadelphus

        Ptolemy III Euergetes I

        Ptolemy IV Philopator

        Ptolemy V Epiphanes

        Ptolemy VI Philometor

        Ptolemy VII Neos Philopator

        Ptolemy VIII Euergetes II

        Ptolemy IX Soter II

        Ptolemy X Alexander I

        Ptolemy XI Alexander II

        Ptolemy XII Neos Dionysos

        Ptolemy XIII and Cleopatra VII

        Ptolemy XIV and Cleopatra VII

        Cleopatra VII

ROMAN EGYPT
30 B.C. to 395 A.D.

In the heart of the Roman Empire, Egypt plays a particular role: on the one hand it is the most important granary of **Rome,** on the other, its privileged position at the crossroads of three continents (Africa, Asia, Europe) gives it a special importance. Contrary to other provinces, Egypt is under the direct authority of the Emperor himself, represented by a prefect. In general, the Roman Emperors adopt the Pharaonic titles; their name, written in hieroglyphics on a cartouche, appears on the walls of the buildings built or reformed under their rule. In reality, although the political change is brutal, culturally and administratively, Egypt retains its own particular character. However, after being resisted for a long time, Christianity triumphs. From 313 A.D. *Constantine* announces certain religious reforms. At the end of the fourth century, *Theodorus* prohibits paganism throughout the Empire and orders the closing of the temples or their transformation into churches.

30 B.C. to 395 A.D. *(the principal Roman Emperors)*

        Augustus

        Tiberius

        Caligula

        Nero

        Trajan

        Hadrian

        Marcus Aurelius

        Septimus Severus

        Caracalla

        Constantine the Great

        Theodorus

BYZANTINE EGYPT
395 to 639

In 395 A.D. Egypt passes under the protection of the Eastern Roman Empire but, rapidly, religious conflicts break out. They are demonstrated by the defeat of the **Monophytes** who refuse the terms of the **Council of Chalcedonia** of 451 and do not delay in forming an indigenous national church called the Coptic Church. The temple of *Isis* at **Philae**, which had escaped the control of the Romans thanks to its remoteness, is finally condemned by *Justinian* in 551; thus paganism disappears from Egypt. As for the Emperors, more occupied in suppressing religious revolts than in the training of their armies, are unable to resist the invaders: when the Persians enter Egypt in 619, they are not met with any resistance. In 629, *Heraclius I* manages to drive out the Persians and seize hold of Mesopotamia but, ten years later, he is defeated by the Arabs.

395 to 639   Arcadius

        Theodorus II

        Marcien

        Leon I

        Zenon

        Anastasius

        Justin

        Justinian

        Justin II

        Tiberius II

        Mauritius

        Phokas

        Heraclius I

MUSLIM EGYPT
639 to 1798

Weary of the Byzantine domination, Egypt only offers a token resistance to the Arab conquerors. In 636, the defeat of the Byzantines in Syria allows the Arab armies to enter Egypt from the **Sinai**: **'Amr ibn el-As,** one of the lieutenants of *'Omar* (second successor of **Muhammad**), conquers **Peluse, Memphis,** the **"Fortress of Babylon"** (the **"Old Cairo"** of today) and founds the town of **Fostat**. In 643, he takes control of **Alexandria** after a long and difficult siege during which the Library of **Alexandria** is consumed by flames. *'Omar* becomes master of the country; Egypt looses its independence and becomes an Arab colony administered by governors named by the Caliphs.

THE UMAYYADS (661 to 750)

In 644, at the death of *'Omar*, two Caliphs succeed him: *Osman* then *'Ali*. Both are assassinated, leaving Mu'awiya, the recently proclaimed Caliph of *Damascus*, to extend his empire over Egypt. He founds the Umayyad dynasty and organizes the country: Arabic becomes the official administrative language, the country is Islamised and **Fostat** grows to become one of the most important centres of the Caliphate. Under pressure from the new conquerors, many Copts adopt the Arabic language and convert to Islam.

THE ABBASSIDS (750 to 870)

In 750, religious conflicts break out leading to the mass elimination of the *Umayyads* in **Damascus**. *Abu al-'Abbas*, descendant of *Al-'Abbas* (*Muhammad*'s uncle), takes advantage of the situation to found the *Abbassid* dynasty and establishes his capital in **Baghdad**. Egypt and Syria enjoy an economic and artistic revival, but the extent of the Empire is such that power is exercised by local chieftains who eagerly found their own independent dynasties in different regions.

THE TULUNIDS (870 to 905)

In Egypt, *Ahmad ibn-Tulun* creates a dynasty that administers the country until 905: the *Tulunid* dynasty. They are the true inaugurators of the artistic history of Muslim Egypt, covering **Cairo** with palaces and mosques. Between 906 and 969, after a struggle that leads to the end of the *Tulunids*, the country is administered from **Baghdad**, then passes to the hands of the *Ikchidits* and, finally, it is conquered by the *Fatimids*.

THE FATIMIDS (969 to 1171)

The *Fatimids*, descendants of *Muhammad*'s daughter *Fatima*, already control almost all of North Africa when, in 969, they found their capital in Egypt. On their arrival, they build, north of **Fostat**, **El-Qahira**, "The Victorious", site of the modern **Cairo**: they build numerous palaces and mosques and found the University of **Al-Azhar**. Egypt becomes the highly developed centre of commercial, economic and cultural exchange. The arrival of the *Crusaders* brings troubles in the heart of the Caliphate which, from now on, will be insecure. For this reason, in answer to the call of the Sultan of **Halap** for assistance, the last *Fatimid* caliph appoints as his vizier the only man capable of fighting against the Franks: *Saladin*.

THE AYYUBIDS (1171 to 1250)

The death of the last caliph allows *Saladin* (or *Salah ad-Din*), founder of the *Ayyubid* dynasty, to unite Egypt and Syria into a single Empire. While his reign is dominated by the struggle against the Franks, he does not neglect the goal of his predecessor, *Nur ad-Din*: to suppress Shi'ism and establish Sunnism. To this end, he founds the **madrasas**, Koranic schools closely controlled by the government. Against the Franks, *Saladin* obtains numerous victories: he recuperates the Syrian possessions while the Latin kingdom is reduced to a narrow costal strip separating **Jaffa** and **Antioch**. However, his descendants, busy with their petty intrigues, end up abandoning the battle against the Franks, who gain new territories by the day. However, in 1250, deprived of supplies and decimated by an epidemic, the Crusaders of *Saint Louis* —the Seventh Crusade— are forced to give up the struggle. Led into a trap, the army is captured and the king is imprisoned in Egypt. For his freedom he gives up **Damietta**; to save his army he pays a ransom. Victorious, the *Mamluks* have only to rid themselves of the last descendant of *Saladin*, *Turan-Shah*, and take power.

THE MAMLUKS (1251 to 1517)

The *Mamluks* possess a very particular organisation within the Muslim world. It consists of a foreign legion, made up of Circassian or Turkish soldiers, supporting a non hereditary power lead by an elected Sultan. At this time, the country is dominated by a strong regime despite numerous internal troubles and power struggles. The Empire extends over Egypt, Syria and Palestine. The *Mamluks* manage to ensure their prosperity thanks to the flow of merchandise between the Orient and the West. Two great dynasties follow one another: The *Mamluks* from Bahrain, toppled in 1382 by *Barquq*, and the Circassian *Mamluks*. In 1517, *Tuman Bey* is chosen as Sultan by the *Mamluks* to save the country and defend it against *Salim I*, the Ottoman sultan, who had seized Syria shortly before. *Salim I* inflicts a terrible defeat on the *Mamluks*; as a sign of victory, *Tuman Bey* is hanged. Egypt loses its independence to become a province of the immense Ottoman Empire.

THE OTTOMANS (1517 to 1798)

Distrustful of the desire for autonomy in the country, *Sulayman II*, called "The Magnificent", sends his vizir *Ibrahim* to **Cairo**. He is to name an administrator, the **pasha**, capable of maintaining a submissive Egypt. The rules are strict. This man will be a foreigner to the country; he will be named by the Ottoman Sultan and will designate the **beys**. However, to avoid any temptation of independence, he will never dispose of Turkish troops whose command is confided to the **agha** of the Janissaries, a colonel of sorts. This system of government is maintained throughout the sixteenth century but the distance from the Sultanate, due to the immensity of the Empire, makes the pasha's authority less and less effective. In reality, power rests more and more in the hands of the **beys** of **Cairo**, often in conflict with each other. For security, certain **beys** depend on militias, amongst which are the *Mamluks* who succeed in becoming again the true masters of the country. When the fleet of *Bonaparte* disembarks in **Alexandria**, in July 12, 1798, the surprise is complete.

COLONIAL EGYPT
1798 to 1952

On arriving in Egypt, *Bonaparte* has several projects in mind: he wants to transform this undisciplined province into a modern state, turned towards the west and revealing to the world the splendours of its glorious past. For this purpose, accompanied by thirty eight thousand men, he brings writers, scientists, engineers, scholars and artists… Besides the awakening of consciousness about the importance of its national past, the French presence in Egypt permits the final rupture with **Istanbul**, even though, officially, the country remains an Ottoman province until 1914. In reality, the circumstances lead *Bonaparte* to give his campaign a more military character than initially foreseen. After three years of struggle against the British-supported Turks, the French army leaves Egypt once a capitulation is signed. Yet again Egypt is in anarchy, victim of the opposing rivalries of the Turks, wishing to re-establish the authority of the sultan of **Istanbul**, and the *Mamluks* who hope to recuperate their ancient prerogatives. As for England, well aware of the importance of Egypt on the route to the Indies, it seeks to guard against an eventual return of

France; to do this, it supports the *Mamluks*. In 1803, the British troops are obliged to withdraw and an Albanian mercenary, *Mehemet Ali*, takes advantage to seize power. After having been named viceroy of Egypt, he undertakes to re-establish order in the country. It is him who brings Egypt into the modern world, imposing reforms which lead to economic and social development. Thanks to the support of France, he obtains hereditary power over Egypt and control of Sudan for life. The status of Egypt becomes somewhat strange: the country remains an Ottoman province, but it is managed by an independent dynasty. *Mehemet Ali* dies in 1849. He leaves behind a colossal achievement: agricultural revolution, creation of industry, furnishing or harbours, reform of administration, organisation of the army and navy, construction of schools, development of health services… After the brief reign of his son *Ibrahim*, *'Abbas I*, his grandson, ascends to the throne. He opposes the reforms undertaken by his predecessor and suppresses all previous administrative and financial arrangements. In 1854, he is assassinated and the seat is left to *Mehemet Sa'id*, the youngest son of *Mehemet Ali*, who resumes the policies of his father. Soon, he authorises *Ferdinand de Lesseps* to found a company for the creation of the **Suez Canal**. In 1857, the French Egyptologist *Mariette* receives the title of **bey** and founds the Museum of Egyptian Antiquities in **Bulaq** which is later transferred to the heart of **Cairo**.

Despite the Anglo-Turkish opposition, the digging of the **Suez Canal** is begun in 1859. In 1863, **Isma'il** succeeds his uncle *Mehemet Sa'id*. His name remains linked to the termination of the **Suez Canal**, inaugurated in November 17, 1869 in a ceremony attended by several famous personalities. However, it does not prevent Egypt from sliding down into a serious economic crisis—in 1875 **Isma'il** is forced to sell his shares of the **Suez** to the British government because he cannot keep up with his financial obligations. Cornered once again a year later, he must accept French-British control over Egyptian finances. Necessarily this decision stirs the anger of the nationalist movement that opposes any foreign intervention in the internal affairs of the country. The situation grows bitterer: in 1882 the British bombard **Alexandria**, occupy **Cairo** and become the only managers of Egyptian affairs. In 1914, Egypt

officially breaks with **Istanbul**. The country becomes a kingdom but looses its freedom since the control becomes official—Britain proclaims a protectorate over Egypt. Quickly, the elites dream of independence and, from 1918, a delegation led by *Sa'd Zaghlul*, manifests its intention to travel to **London** to reclaim independence. Not only is he refused an audience, but he is also arrested and deported to **Malta**. The reaction is immediate: riots break out in **Cairo**. They intensify and become more and more violent until in 1922 Britain declares Egypt a "sovereign and independent country". **Fu'ad I**, now sultan, declares himself king of Egypt and promulgates a Constitution. However, the control and occupation persist; in fact, the situation remains unchanged. The **Wafd** party, created by *Sa'ad Zaghlul*, seeks to find a common ground with the British. Agreements are signed in 1936-37, while *Faruq* succeeds his father: the country regains its financial independence and is admitted to the League of Nations. The war obliges numerous British companies to close up: the ensuing inflation and unemployment reveal the latent social tensions. Riots and assassination attempts occur; the situation quickly degenerates. In 1952, a group of British massacre a company of Egyptian policemen. The next day, a riot breaks out in **Cairo**; amidst cries for vengeance, the city is fought for by fire and sword. The **Wafd** is not able to intervene; power falls into the hands of young officers led by General *Nagib* and *Faruq* abdicates in favour of his son, *Fu'ad II*.

REPUBLICAN EGYPT
since 1952
GAMAL 'ABD AN-NASSER

In 1953, the monarchy is abolished, the republic is proclaimed and the first five-year plan is launched. Rapidly, *Nagib* is dismissed from his duties in favour of *Nasser*, who from now on takes all of the reigns of power. In 1956, when the last British soldier has left the country, *Nasser* officially becomes President of the Republic. Shortly after, in face of the categorical refusal of the United States to finance the **Aswan Dam**, he nationalises the Universal **Suez Canal** Company. Its revenues are such that they will finance the construction of the dam. This displeases **London**, **Paris** and **Jerusalem** who launch a military offensive immediately condemned by the United Nations: *Nasser*, re-enforced by this venture, becomes the uncontested leader of the

Arab world and non-aligned countries. In 1965, he is triumphantly re-elected. In his role as leader of the Arab Nation, he must pursue his struggle against Israel. However, Israeli threats against Syria encourage him to order the blockade of the **Strait of Tiran**. Israel attacks and scores a clear victory over the Egyptian troops in the *"Six-Day War"*. *Nasser* offers his resignation, but the protests in **Cairo** keep him in power. Israel occupies the **Sinai** and the **Suez Canal** is from now on closed for navigation. In September, 28 1970, *Nasser* dies; the Arab world is grief-stricken.

ANWAR ES-SADAT

From the beginning, *Sadat* launches a new policy: he seeks to turn towards the West and towards the new Gulf States. Aiming to liberalise the market, he takes the risk of destabilising the middle classes on whom the government of *Nasser* depended; he thinks he can compensate for this by the acceleration of development. In this perspective, peace with Israel is imposed; in 1973, the *"Yom Kippur War"* permits Egyptian forces to cross the **Suez Canal** and free a part of the Sinai; the war yields no real winner or loser, but it opens the door to negotiations. In 1975, exactly eight years after its closure, the **Suez Canal** is solemnly opened to navigation. In 1977 *Sadat* travels to **Jerusalem** to initiate the talks; this initiative costs him a rupture with the rest of the Arab world. At the peace conference held in **Cairo** in December of the same year, only Egypt, Israel, the United States and the United Nations are represented. In 1978 the first agreements are signed at **Camp David**. They announce the Israeli-Egyptian peace treaty, signed in March 26, 1979 in **Washington**: jointly, *Sadat* and *Begin* receive the Nobel peace prize. At the same time, the country experiences the difficulties linked to the demands of its economic development and the consequences of its galloping demographics. The relations with the West intensify and foreign capital, searching for profitable investments, begins to flow in. A policy for the development of infrastructure is put in place and great efforts are made towards education and training. Although re-elected in 1976, *Sadat* is assassinated by Muslim fanatics. He is succeeded by *Hosni Mubarak*, who leads the country towards the twenty-first century knowing how to maintain Egypt's strategic place on the world stage.

DIVINITIES

AMUN - He originally comes from **Thebes**, but becomes the national and dynastic god from the Middle Kingdom on. His main place of worship is in **Thebes** (**Luxor** and **Karnak**) where he is venerated with the goddess *Mut* and the god son *Khons*.

ANUBIS - This funerary god, depicted as a jackal or as a jackal-headed man, is supposed to be the inventor of mummification and, therefore, makes sure the embalming ceremonies are properly conducted. He is the protector of the necropolis.

ANUKIS - She is the infant goddess of the **Elephantine** triad. With the god *Khnum* and the goddess *Satis*, she is guardian of the sources of the Nile and patroness of the cataract.

APIS - The sacred bull from **Memphis** is considered to be the representative of *Ptah* on Earth. He is sometimes associated with *Osiris* and *Ra*; in this case, he adopts funerary and solar characteristics. The sacred bulls are buried in particular necropolis called **Serapeum**.

ATEN - Solar god par excellence, given the rank of dynastic divinity by *Akhenaten*.

BASTET - This cat goddess, worshipped in the Delta at **Bubastis**, is the incarnation of the peaceful aspects of the dangerous goddesses.

HAPY - He represents the inundation and the flood of the Nile, which guarantee the fertility of cultivated fields. As a symbol of plenty, *Hapy* is depicted as an androgynous deity, sometimes female and sometimes male, with hanging breasts.

HARMAKHIS - *"Horus on the Horizon"* is a solar deity represented by the Sphinx of **Giza**.

HAROERIS - *"Horus the Great"* is the falcon god from **Kom Ombo**, who fights against the enemies of *Ra*. In certain traditions, he is related to the cosmogony of **Heliopolis**, where he is *"Horus the Elder,"* one of the five children of *Geb* and *Nut*.

HATHOR - She is one of the most popular goddesses of the Egyptian pantheon. She is goddess of beauty, love and joy, patroness of the Theban necropolis, celestial deity, mistress of the foreign lands, and nurse of the royal child.

HEQET - This goddess with a frog's head, is associat-ed, in **Antinoe**, with the potter and creative god, *Khnum*.

HORUS - He is the son of *Isis* and *Osiris*, who inherits from his grandfather, the god *Geb*, the kingdom of Earth. *Horus* is the main dynastic god, and the pharaohs are under his direct protection. He is also a solar and a celestial god; as such, he is associated with the goddess *Hathor* who is his wife.

ISIS - She is wife and sister of *Osiris*, mother of *Horus*, and she has a very strong personality that confers many roles on her: protector of women and children, great magician, protector of the mummy of the deceased, universal goddess…

KHNUM - This god with a ram's head has several places of worship: in **Elephantine** as the god of the cataract and the guardian of the sources of the Nile, in triad with *Satis* and *Anukis*; in **Esna**, he is the creative god. It is told that, on his potter's wheel, he has fashioned gods, nature, men and objects.

Khons - He is in direct relation with the moon. In the 18th Dynasty, he is associated with the god *Amun* and the goddess *Mut* as the son god of the Theban triad.

MIN - He is the god of fertility associated, in this role, with *Amun*, the god of the Kingdom. He is worshipped in **Koptos** and **Akhmim** as protector of the caravans and patron of the oriental desert tracks.

MONTU - He is a falcon god from **Thebes**, who incarnates the irresistible force of war.

MUT - In **Thebes**, this vulture goddess is the divine consort of *Amun* and the mother of the god *Khons*. She sometimes adopted the features of the warrior lion goddesses as *Sakhmet*.

NEITH - She has several functions: she is the warrior goddess of the town of **Sais** and demiurge of the town of **Esna**. In the underground world, she protects the **canopic jars** of the deceased with *Isis*, *Nephthys* and *Serket*.

NEKHBET - She is the vulture goddess of **el-Kab**, patroness of Upper Egypt.

NEPHTHYS - She belongs to the gods of the Heliopolitan Ennead, with *Osiris, Isis, Horus the Elder* and *Seth*. Her role is essentially funerary, as she watches over the body of the deceased.

NUN - He is the primeval ocean that precedes creation in the cosmogonies and represents nothingness: *"before the existence of the sky, before the existence of the earth, before the existence of men, before the existence of death"* was *Nun*.

NUT - She is the representation of the celestial vault. In the Heliopolitan cosmogony, she forms with *Geb*, the Earth, the second divine couple. The day and night journey of the sun are made on her body, which is the symbol of the space through which the Sun travels.

OSIRIS - He is the god of the dead in the Egyptian pantheon, who also represents, because of his resurrection, the yearly revival of vegetation. Everyone tries to identify himself with *Osiris* in the afterworld, and to enter his kingdom, since he is the only one who can give hope of eternal life.

PTAH - At the beginning, he is the patron of goldsmiths, sculptors and craftsmen; he is considered as the inventor of technical skills. Afterwards, he becomes the creative god of **Memphis** in the triad where he is the husband of *Sakhmet* and the father of *Nefertem*. In time he merges with *Sokar* and *Osiris* to form *Ptah-Sokar-Osiris*, and with *Tanen* to form *Ptah-Tanen*.

RA - He is pre-eminently the solar god, the most important deity of the Egyptian Pantheon. His main place of worship is in **Heliopolis**, but he is venerated throughout Egypt under many names: *Ra-Harakhty, Amun-Ra, Ra-Atum, Sobek-Ra...*

SAKHMET - She is a power of destruction, incarnating the solar eye and dangerous forces. She is depicted as a goddess with the head of a lioness. She belongs to the Memphite triad, wife of *Ptah* and mother of *Nefertem*. In **Thebes**, she is assimilated with the goddess *Mut* as a healing goddess.

SARAPIS - The pharaohs of the Greek period created this god in **Alexandria** to help the interests of the new political regime. He is the protector of the ptolemaic dynasty and of the town of **Alexandria**. He also has agrarian and funerary functions, and was the healing god of the kingdom.

SATIS - She is both guardian of the sources of the Nile and patroness of the cataract, associated with *Khnum* and *Anukis*.

SETH - This god with the head of a mythical animal has many facets, some positive and some negative. He is at the same time the protector of the sun boat, and the murderer of *Osiris*.

SOBEK - The crocodile god has several places of worship, the most famous ones being in the region of **Fayum** and in **Kom Ombo**. In certain cases he is the creative god, but he is most often a protector of men against wild beasts and hostile forces that live in the marshes and the waters of the Nile.

TAWERET - She has no particular place of worship, but is venerated in all Egyptian households as goddess protector of pregnant women and children.

THOTH - He is sometimes depicted as an ibis and sometimes as a baboon. He has many functions and many powers: he is the moon god, the inventor of writing and science, the protector of scribes, the master of knowledge, the divine messenger and bookkeeper. In the afterworld, he is responsible for the proper weighing of hearts, and he writes down the verdict on the sacred scriptures.

WADJIT - She is the cobra goddess of **Buto**, patroness of Lower Egypt.

LEXICON

AKH - It is one of the spiritual principles that composes human personality. The **akh** is considered to be an immortal principle, a kind of invisible power that can lend its efficiency to mankind. In certain contexts, **akh** applies to the privileged deceased, to spectres or to "spirits", certain divinities that are half way between the gods and mankind.

AKHET - This word refers to the first season of the Egyptian year: the **flood**. It takes place from June to October.

AMULETS - These objects are little figurines serving to protect the living and the dead. Living Egyptians wear amulets as pendants, and the deceased have them placed in their linen wrappings. They are made of earthenware, precious or semi-precious stone, bronze, gold, silver… They either represent divinities or hieroglyphic signs full of meaning: the **djed** pillar (longevity and stability), the **ankh** cross (life), the **wedjat** eye (plenty), the **kheper** dung beetle (existence) or the **girdle of Isis** (protection in all circumstances).

BA - Represented as a human-headed bird, the **ba**, the soul of the deceased in certain ways, is a spiritual entity that leaves the body when death takes over and finds its individuality to roam at its leisure. The **ba** can stay in the tomb near the body, go into the funerary chapel to appreciate the offerings or, even, go out into the fresh air to visit the deceased's favourite places once again.

BEY - This name bears a Turkish origin that carries the meaning of "Master" and designates a superior official or a high post from the times of the *Mamluks*.

BOOK OF THE DEAD - Appearing from the New Kingdom on, this collection of texts, more correctly called the **"Book for coming forth by day"**, is a loose group of recipes that are supposed to secure the revival of the deceased in the afterworld, giving him complete freedom of movement and giving him everything he needs in the underworld. The chapters, very often decorated with illustrations and vignettes, are written on a papyrus scroll, put into the coffin or inserted in the linen wrappings of the mummy. Many copies of this funerary book have been found, but they are all different, some have chapters that do not exist in others. To this day, there have been 190 different chapters recorded; they are numbered from I to CXC.

CANOPIC JARS - The mummified viscera of the deceased are preserved in four canopic jars, made out of alabaster or limestone, and put under the protection of four gods, called the *four sons of Horus*, and four goddesses. *Hapy*, with a baboon's head, and *Nephthys* watch over the lungs; *Imset*, with a man's head, and *Isis* watch over the liver; *Qebehsenuf*, with a falcon's head, and *Serket* watch over the intestines; *Duamutef*, with a jackal's head, and *Neith* watch over the stomach.

CARTOUCHE - This word designates the elongated buckle symbolizing the universal reign of the king, and encircling the fourth and fifth names of the pharaohs: the **"Throne"** name (or **"He of the sedge and the bee"**) and the **"Birth"** name (or **"Son of Ra"**).

CHADOUF - It refers to an hydraulic balancing mechanism used in Egypt from Ancient times to irrigate the land and to collect water from a well.

CLAUSTRA - In Egypt, this system of construction consisted in creating a difference in the level of the ceiling and in making a hole situated between these two levels in order allow light to enter.

COFFIN TEXTS - As opposed to the **"Pyramid texts"**, only reserved to the royal person, these funerary texts are used by civilians and decorate the coffins during the Middle Kingdom. Issued from the democratisation of the funerary creeds, they allow the deceased to identify himself to *Osiris* in the afterworld, through spells and recipes aimed to deify the deads.

CONSORT - This word is used to qualify a goddess who is considered to be the wife of a god in a sanctuary. In the Theban triad, the goddess *Mut* is the consort of *Amun*, in the Elephantine triad, the goddess *Satis* is the consort of *Khnum*…

COSMOGONY - It is a mythic tale describing the creation of the world and the settling of the natural elements of the universe: earth, sky, stars… Many religious centers have their own cosmogonic legend: **Heliopolis, Memphis, Esna, Thebes, Crocodilopolis, Hermopolis**… Each one has a creative god, called "demiurge", who conceives his creation with his own means; for example, it is said that *Ptah* creates "by his thought and his tongue" and *Khnum* shapes the gods, the human beings and the objects on his potter's wheel.

DROMOS - The Greeks gave this name to the alley that extends the axis of a temple, towards the outside, to link it to another one or to a landing on the Nile. These alleys are often bordered with sphinxes or recumbent lions.

EMBALMENT - There is a very precise logic behind the invention and use of the techniques for mummification. In Egypt, death is not the end, but a passage to another form of existence. But, this passage is very dangerous because during the period of dying, the different elements of the human personality (the **ka**, the **ba**, the name, the body, the heart…) separate, each one keeping its own integrity. If they can all be gathered together, a second life is possible; and so, everything is done to preserve the body, since if it is damaged, all chance of another life fades away. The embalming has to preserve the body. The technique consists in taking the entrails out of the body, before putting it in a bath of natron for seventy days to dehydrate it. The body is washed afterwards, perfumed, and wrapped in linen, with inserted amulets. The viscera are mummified apart and kept in the four **canopic jars** protected by the *four Sons of Horus* (*Imset, Duamutef, Qebehsenuf* and *Hapy*).

FELLAH - This word designates the countrymen and has an Arabian origin. It is also applied to the countrymen of ancient times.

GALABIEH - It refers to that long and ample robe worn by men in Arabian countries.

HADJ - It is the designation given to the Muslims pilgrims who have reached **Mecca**.

HYPOGEUM - This word designates a tomb, either royal or civilian, dug into a cliff.

HYPOSTYLE - This refers to a room where the ceiling is supported by columns.

IB - It is the hieroglyphic word that means heart.

KA - This notion is difficult to understand for there is no concept in our language for the Egyptian **ka**. It is considered to be a manifestation of the life force, either conservative or creative, that continues to live after the death of the body. Offerings and funerary formulas are addressed to the **ka**, which is the element allowing the deceased to survive in the afterworld.

KHET - It is the hieroglyphic word that means the material body.

KUSH (LAND OF) - At the beginning of the Pharaonic history, the land of **Kush** referred to a small region of Nubia that was situated to the South of the Second Cataract. Consequently, it includes the group of Nubian territories. During the Old Kingdom, the region located between **el-Kab** and the Fourth Cataract was under a Viceroy, the "royal son of **Kush**", and was divided in two domains: **Wawat** in the North and **Kush** in the South.

LEGEND OF OSIRIS - It is the most famous legend of Egyptian literature. Unfortunately, only the Greek writer **Plutarch** gives a complete version of this story in his *De Iside a Osiride*. The Egyptian texts are very mutilated and have many gaps. This legend of Heliopolitan tradition recalls the three periods in the life of the gods from the great Ennead: the murder of *Osiris* by *Seth*, the birth and childhood of *Horus* and the struggle between *Horus* and *Seth* for the kingdom of earth.

MADRASA - Nowadays, this Arabian word just means "school". In ancient times, it designated the Koranic centres of learning founded by the *Ayyubids* to teach Sunni.

MAMMISI - Of Copt origin, this word is literally translated as "birthplace". It refers to those buildigs annexed to the temples of the Late period, where the Egyptians celebrated the birth rituals of the Child gods (*Nefertem, Khons…*) every year, and by extension boy king.

MELAYEH - This Arabian words refers to the black veil women cover themselves with when going outside.

MONOPHYSISM - This religious doctrine that dates from the fifth century has its origin in the refusal of the **Chalcedonies Council** formulations in the year 451. **Monophysism** only believes in one of Christ's natures whereas the Council believes he is both god and man, that is one person with two natures. This schism brought on the creation of many orthodox Religions: Coptic religion, Armenian religion, Ethiopian religion…

NAOS - It has two meanings: the stone tabernacle in which the statue of the god was placed, as well as the enclosed shrine areas that were reserved for statues in ancient Egyptian temples.

NARGUILÉ - This Arabian word refers to the water pipe that is used in the Orient. It is made up of a cylinder attached to a bottle full of water with a long flexible tube.

NOME - It is the name given by the Greeks to the administrative constituency of the Nile Valley. After thirty centuries, the name, the limits and the designation of these nomes haven't stopped evolving due to social and political reforms. Whatever the era, the nome has always been an economic and legal entity, made up by temples, gods and laws that must be respected by all.

NORIA - It refers to the hydraulic mechanism composed of a big wheel with multiple buckets that are plunged in empty and bring out full. In Egypt, the noria has been used since Ancient times. It used to be worked by an animal, but has been replaced by a motor.

NUBIA - This geographical zone stretches from the city of **Khartoum**, now the capital of Sudan, to the city of **Aswan**. During the pharaonic period, Nubia was totally dominated by Egypt and used only as a source of gold, wood, stone, cattle and manpower and as a transit zone for the riches from Africa: ivory, ebony, rare animals and essential oils.

OPET (FEAST OF) - This feast was celebrated on the day of the Egyptian new year, in the second month of the flood. Although it was probably observed all over Egypt, our source of information is the detailed accounts of it from the great temple at **Karnak**. The gods of the Theban triad, *Amun, Mut* and *Khons*, were brought up the Nile to the temple of **Luxor**, the "Southern Harem" amid cheering crowds who chanted incantations and offered them food and donations. The festivities lasted for about ten days, during which there were not only the ritual celebrations, but also oracles by *Amun* concerning problems and dilemmas that had proved insoluble.

At the end of the celebrations, the gods returned to their principal residence at **Karnak** by the same route.

OSTRACON - Because of its cost, papyrus was reserved for official or religious use; therefore, private letters or texts, personal notes, rough drafts and outlines were made on less noble materials, such as pottery shards or limestone chips. These documents are called **ostracon**. Some of them are very valuable as they give us quite detailed information of the daily life of the ancient Egyptians: for example, those found at **Deir el-Medina**, the village inhabited by the men working in the **Valley of the Kings** during the New Kingdom.

PACHA - For the *Ottomans*, it was an honorific title given to the governor of Egypt. Generally it refers to the man who carries out important duties.

POUNT (LAND OF) - The precise geographical situation of the land of Pount is unknown; but in all probability it must correspond to Somalia or Yemen. Wherever it may be, it is a region in which the Egyptians searched for their incense, gold, fragrances and strange animals,...

PYLON -This element of architecture marks the monumental entrance to a temple. A pylon is composed of two massive trapezoidal piles flanking the gate that gives access to the cult site. Very often, their fronts are decorated with pictures of a pharoah of heroic proportions offering to the god a handful of enemies whom he clutches by their hair.

PYRAMID TEXTS - They are the funerary texts engraved on the walls of the pyramids built at the end of the Old Kingdom. The oldest text goes back to the time of *Unas,* the last king of the 5th Dynasty. All the kings of the 6th Dynasty had them inscribed, but they disappear with the unrest of the First Intermediate Period. Magical spells, different hymns and religious incantations are supposed to secure the king immortality and to allow him to unite with the Sun.

REN - This hieroglyphic term is the "name" that exists as the second creation of the being. Egyptians strongly believed in the creative virtues of names: giving a person a name made him exist even after the disappearance of the physical body.

SACRED ANIMALS - The Egyptians think that any animal is the receptacle of a part of the divine power, whether good or bad. This explains the large number of cults of sacred animals: the crocodile (god *Sobek*), the ibis or the baboon (god *Thoth*), the cat (goddess *Bastet*), the bull (god *Apis*), the falcon (god *Horus*), and the jackal (god *Anubis*) are the main ones.

SACRED LAKE - Every entire cultural ensemble is made up of, apart from the buildings necessary for religious ceremonies, a rectangular (or other shaped) pond, the access into which is by various sets of steps. In these waters, priests ritually purified themselves and sacred boats floated. Above all it was supposed to resemble the Original Ocean where life itself originated.

SAKH - This hieroglyphic word designates the spiritual body.

SEBAKH - It is an Arabian word that applies to the earth that is used as manure and consists of the waste found in ancient sites (biological and mineral debris).

SEKHEM - It is the hieroglyphic word that designates spiritual energy.

SERDAB - The **serdab** is that part which is dug into the superstructure of the mastaba and which contains the statue of **ka**, god of the dead. Completely closed off, the funeral chapel was reached by means of a small opening, which was used by the relations of the deceased to leave offerings for the enjoyment of the statue.

SPEOS - By this, we are referring to the sanctuary dug into a cliff face. The most beautiful example of this type of construction, is that which *Ramesses II* built in **Abu Simbel**, 200 miles south of **Aswan**.

SPHINX - This lion with a human head, called the sphinx, is in general the symbol of the king or a Sun god. As the incarnation of the king, it is supposed to fight against enemies and to protect men. As representative of the Sun god on Earth, it watches over the western regions, which the deceased and the sun leave. The sphinx of **Giza** belongs to this second category of sphinxes: it incarnates *Harmakhis*, *"Horus on the Horizon"* and *Hurun*, the god assimilated into *Harmakhis* from the New Kingdom.

STELA - It is a monolithic slab, usually of limestone, on which can be engraved different inscriptions: decrees, official announcements, funerary formulas, lists of offerings. Sometimes these stelae are memorials. They are votive offerings that the faithful put into the sanctuaries, after having made a pilgrimage to a holy place, or to thank the god of a temple for having made a wish come true.

TRIAD - It is a group of three deities of the same town, in a family structure: god, goddess, god son or goddess daughter. The most famous triads are the triad of **Memphis** with *Ptah, Sakhmet* and *Nefertem*, the triad of **Thebes** with *Amun, Mut* and *Khons*, the triad of **Elephantine** with *Khnum, Satis* and *Anukis* and the triad of **Abydos** with *Osiris, Isis* and *Horus*.

URAEUS - This word designates the cobra with the extended hood, the eye of *Ra* of the Heliopolitan legend, topping the royal headdress. It is said that he protects the king everywhere under any circumstances *"even during the night when he sleeps"*, and he repels all the enemies of Pharaoh.

USHABTI (SHABTI or **SHAWABTI)** - Put in the tomb, this mummiform figurine has, in the underworld, to do all the daily tasks for the deceased. A few words are carved on them: *"O Ushabti! If X (the deceased) is required to do one of the tasks in the next world… You will say: Here I am!"* Appearing during the Middle Kingdom, the ushabties are made, according to the status of the deceased, of wood, bronze, earthenware, stone or terra-cotta.

BIOGRAPHIES

ACHILLES - Son of *Peleus* and *Thetis*, and the Illiad's main character; killer of Ethiopian King *Memnon* during the **Trojan war**.

AESCHYLUS - 525/524-456/455 B.C. Greek tragic poet whose plays are inspired by ancient legends and myths.

AMANITORE- Spouse of *Natakamani*, King of **Meroe**.

ARISTOTLE - 384-332 B.C. Greek philosopher; tutor of *Alexander the Great* and author of numberless scientific works.

ARKAMANI - King of **Meroe** ruling over Nubia between 218 B.C. and 200 B.C. One of the builders of the temple of **Dakka**, which nowadays stands on the shore of **Lake Nasser**.

BAKER, SAMUEL - 1821-1893 English explorer; discoverer of **Lake Albert** (Zaire) in 1864.

BONAPARTE, NAPOLEON - 1769-1821 Emperor of France (1804-1814, and 1815); commanding the French expedition to Egypt, he arrives in **Alexandria** in July 12, 1798 with numerous scholars. All data collected during the campaign is published in 1809 and in 1822 in a work named *La Description de l'Egypte.*

BRUCE, JAMES - 1730-1794 Scottish explorer who travelled in Ethiopia searching for the sources of the Blue Nile. His rambling, at times barely plausible, five-volumed account, *Travels to Discover the Sources of the Nile 1768-1774*, is nevertheless an essential guide to Ethiopian history.

BURTON, RICHARD - 1821-1890 English traveller; discoverer of **Lake Tanganyika** (Zaire, Tanzania) in 1865.

CARTER, HOWARD - 1874-1939 English Egyptologist; discoverer of the tomb of Pharaoh *Tuthankhamun* in the **Valley of the Kings**, in 1922.

CHAMPOLLION, JEAN-FRANÇOIS - 1790-1832 French Egyptologist; discoverer, in 1822, of the system for deciphering hieroglyphics.

DAVIS, THEODORE - 1837-1915 American Egyptologist; discoverer of the tomb of *Tuya* and *Yuya* (1905), Queen *Tiy*'s parents, and of the so-called "**Tomb 55**" or **KV 55** (1907), both located in the **Valley of the Kings**.

DINKA - Nilotic people inhabiting the Sudanese province of **Bahr el-Ghazal**, in the White Nile valley.

DIODORUS SICULUS - Circa first century B.C. Greek historian and author of a *Bibliotheca Historica* with a first volume devoted to Egypt.

EOS - Goddess of dawn and mother of heroic king *Memnon*.

FATHER PAEZ - Portuguese missionary who in 1618 discovered the sources of the Blue Nile in **Lake Tana**, Ethiopia.

GONEIM, ZAKARIA - 1911-1959 Egyptian Egyptologist; discoverer of the pyramid complex of *Sekhemkhet*.

HERODOTUS - 484?-430/20? B.C. Greek historian and traveller, author of the History, whose Book II is devoted to Egypt.

HOMER - circa 850 B.C. ? Greek epic poet, presumed author of the *Illiad* and the *Odissey*.

LAUER, JEAN-PHILIPPE - b. 1902 French archaeologist working since 1926 in *Djoser*'s funerary complex at **Saqqara**.

LIVINGSTONE, DAVID - 1813-1873 English missionary and explorer. Over the course of his many travels in Africa, he searched to locate the sources of the Nile.

MANETHON - circa 300 B.C. Egyptian priest and historian, author of the *Aegyptiaca* which included a list of Egypt's Pharaohs classified in empires and dynasties, from *Narmer* to *Ptolemy II*.

MARIETTE, AUGUSTE - 1821-1881 French Egyptologist, discoverer of the **Serapeum** of **Memphis**; besides working in the most important archaeological sites of Egypt and Nubia, he also founded the **Egyptian Museum of Cairo**, devoted to Pharaonic history.

MASPERO, GASTON - 1846-1916 French Egyptologist, successor of *Mariette* as director of the Department of Antiquities in the **Egyptian Museum of Cairo**. In 1881 he discovered in **Deir el Bahri** a cache of royal mummies from the New Kingdom.

MEHEMET ALI (MUHAMMAD 'ALI) - 1769-1849 Viceroy of Egypt (1805-1848).

MEMNON - Hero killed by *Achilles* and assimilated by the ancient Greeks to the colossi of *Amenhotep II* at **West Thebes**.

MONTET, PIERRE - 1885-1966 French Egyptologist who devoted all his life to studying the site of **Tanis**. In 1939 he discovered the royal necropolis containing the tombs of certain 21st and 22nd Dynasties Paharaohs.

MORGAN, JACQUES DE - 1857-1924 Archaeologist who conducted numerous excavations at different sites and who discovered in 1894, at **Dahshur**, superb jewellery from the Middle Kingdom.

MUBARAK, HOSNI - b. 1928 President of the Arab Republic of Egypt since 1981.

NASSER, GAMAL ABDEL - 1918/1970 President of the Arab Republic of Egypt (1956-1970).

NATAKAMANI - King of **Meroe** ruling over Nubia between 12 B.C. and 12 A.D.; after the sack of **Napata** by the armies of Petronius, he had a palace built at the foot of **Gebel Barkal** as well as temples dedicated to the lion *Apedemak* and to *Amun,* at **Naga**.

NUER - Nilotic people living south of the *Shilluk*, in Sudan's White Nile Valley.

PETRIE, W. M. FLINDERS - 1853-1942 British Egyptologist and acknowledged as the alltime chief scholar in the field of Egyptian archaeology; he conducted excavations in most of Egypt's major sites.

PTOLEMY, CLAUDIUS - circa 100-170 Ancient Greek mathematician, astronomer and geographer, author of a *Guide to Geography,* used until the Renaissance, and a *Mathematical Collection,* a corpus of ancient astronomical knowledge.

REISNER, GEORGES A. - 1867-1942 American Egyptologist who engaged in numerous excavations in Egypt and Nubia: **Giza**, **Kerma**, royal necropolis of **Kush**…

SADAT, ANWAR EL - 1918-1981 President of the Arab Republic of Egypt (1970-1981), assassinated in 1981 by Muslim radicals.

SPEKE, JOHN HANNING - 1827-1864 English explorer, first European to visit **Lake Victoria** (Tanzania, Kenya, Uganda), source of the White Nile.

SHILLUK - Nilotic people living in Sudan's **Malakal** province, on the western bank of the White Nile. The *Shilluk* are descendants from the first Nilotic tribe that settled on the region and are ruled by a king.

STANLEY, JOHN ROWLANDS - 1841-1904 British-American journalist and explorer sent by the *New York Herald* to search for *Livingstone*; he definitively settled the problem of the Nile sources by confirming that the White Nile rose in **Lake Victoria**, and by locating the two peaks whose snow feed the great lakes of Central Africa: *Claudius Ptolemy*'s *Mountains of the Moon,* **Peak Margaret** and **Peak Alexandra**, locally known as the **Ruwenzori**.

VYSE, RICHARD HOWARD - 1784-1853 English Egyptologist renowned for his work on Old Kingdom necropolis —**Dahshur, Abu Rawash, Giza**…).

BIBLIOGRAPHY

Cyril Aldred,
The Egyptians, Thames and Hudson, London / New York, 1961 / 1984

John Baines et Jaromir Malek,
Atlas of Ancient Egypt, Andromeda, Oxford, 1980 and 1996

Paul Barguet,
Le Livre des Morts des Anciens Égyptiens - Les Textes des Sarcophages des Égyptiens du Moyen Empire (two volumes),
Cerf, Littérature Ancienne du Proche Orient (LAPO), 1967 and 1986

Maria Carmela Betró,
Hiéroglyphes, les mystères de l'écriture, Flammarion, 1995

Peter A. Clayton,
Chronicle of the Pharaohs,
Thames and Hudson, London, 1994 and 1999

Marc Collier and Bill Manley,
How to read Egyptian hieroglyphs,
British Museum Press, London, 1998 and 1999

Christiane Desroches-Noblecourt,
Toutankhamon, vie et mort d'un pharaon, Pygmalion, 1988

Christiane Desroches-Noblecourt,
Amours et fureur de la Lointaine, Stock, Paris, 1995

Mircea Eliade,
Traité d'histoire des religions, Payot, Paris, 1987

Raymond O. Faulkner,
The Ancient Egyptian Book of the Dead,
under the management of C. Andrews, London, 1985 and 1996

Raymond O. Faulkner,
The Ancient Egyptian Pyramid Texts (two volumes), Oxford, 1969

Henri Frankfort,
Ancient Egyptian Religion, New York, 1948

Sir Allan Gardiner,
Egypt of the Pharaohs, Oxford / New York, 1961

John Gwyn Griffiths,
The conflict of Horus and Seth from Egyptian and Classical sources,
Liverpool, 1960

John Gwyn Griffiths,
Plutarch's De Iside et Osiride, Swansea, 1970

Nicolas Grimal,
Histoire de l'Égypte ancienne, Fayard, 1988

George Hart,
Egyptian myths, British Museum Press

William C. Hayes,
The scepter of Egypt. A background for the study of the Egyptian Antiquities in the Metropolitan Museum of Art. Part 2,
Metropolitan Museum of Art, New York, 1959

Herodotus,
Histories, Book II, A. B. Lloyd,
Herodotus Book II.1: an intoduction (Leiden, 1975)
Herodotus Book II.2: commentary 1-98 (Leiden, 1976)
Herodotus Book II.2: commentary 99-182 (Leiden, 1988)

Erik Hornung,
Der Eine und die Vielen, Darmstadt, 1971

Claire Lalouette,
Textes sacrés et textes profanes de l'Ancienne Égypte,
Connaissances de l'Orient, Gallimard UNESCO, Paris, 1984

Mark Lehner,
The complete Pyramids, Thames and Hudson, London

Dimitri Meeks et Christine Favard-Meeks,
La vie quotidienne des dieux égyptiens, Hachette, 1993

Siegfried Morenz,
Osiris und Amun, Kult und Heilige Stätten, Munich, 1966

Georges Posener, Serge Sauneron et Jean Yoyotte,
Dictionnaire de la civilisation égyptienne, Hazan, 1959

Donald B. Redford,
Akhenaton, the heretic king, Princeton, 1995

Nicholas Reeves,
The complete Tutankhamun, Thames and Hudson, London, 1990

Nicholas Reeves and Richard H. Wilkinson,
The complete Valley of the Kings, Thames and Hudson, London

Serge Sauneron et Jean Yoyotte,
La naissance du monde selon l'Égypte ancienne,
Sources Orientales I, Seuil, Paris, 1959

Ian Shaw et Paul Nicholson,
British Museum, Dictionary of Ancient Egypt,
British Museum Press, 1995

Jacques Vandier,
Manuel d'archéologie égyptienne (six volumes de texte et deux volumes de planches), Éditions A. et J. Picard & Cie, Paris, 1952 à 1964

Jacques Vandier,
La religion égyptienne, Paris, P.U.F., Collection "Mana", 1949